These books available at
NORTHWESTERN
BOOK STORE
20 So. 11th St., Minneapolis, Minn.

Footprints of God

By
ARTHUR I. BROWN, M.D., F.R.C.S.Ed.

Scientist, Lecturer, and Author of, "God and You, Wonders of the Human Body," "God's Creative Forethought," "Men, Monkeys and Missing Links," "What of the Night?" "Into the Clouds," etc., etc.

Foreword by
CHARLES M. A. STINE, Ph.D., Sc.D., LL.D.

Printed in U. S. A.

Published by
FUNDAMENTAL TRUTH
PUBLISHERS
P. O. Box 388   Findlay, Ohio

Copyright 1943

FUNDAMENTAL TRUTH PUBLISHERS

DEDICATION

This Book Is Dedicated to My Dear Friend
GERALD MARTIN FENNELL
*Whose Christian Fellowship Is So Sincerely
Appreciated by the Author*

FOOTPRINTS OF GOD

FOREWORD

To those of us who are familiar with the writings of Dr. Brown another product of his fine mind and consecrated pen is a rare treat. It is only infrequently that such a combination of spiritual insight and trained familiarity with a subject are brought to bear upon the ramparts of agnostic materialism and the trenches of atheistic modernism.

This gifted Christian scholar writes with unusual facility and in most interesting fashion of scientific developments, and the accumulated knowledge resulting from scientific research and study in the field of the natural sciences. His style is both lucid and succinct.

By those of us who have read and re-read his book, "God and You," the reading of this latest work of Dr. Brown, "Footprints of God," will be especially eagerly looked forward to. The reading and study of such books as these do much to engender, in the heart and mind of the reader, humility, reverence, faith and love for his Creator. Such books as these, by an author of Dr. Brown's ability and spiritual vision, assist to an important degree to combat the all too prevalent cynical, materialistic and crassly worldly viewpoint of today's so-called literature.

Science without God is comparable to a storm of great hailstones, but science interwoven with Christian faith is comparable to the warm, gentle shower of a summer afternoon with a rainbow in the sky. One may spread death and destruction, the other life and growth. The effects produced are not unlike, if you will meditate upon them. In the same fashion Dr. Brown's fine Christian approach to the scientific matters of which he writes refresh the heart and mind of the reader and nurture his Christian life and faith. I wish, especially, that every young person might have the opportunity to become familiar with Dr. Brown's writings. I highly and urgently recommend them to my own friends and acquaintances, particularly the young people, upon every opportunity to do so.

The chemist determines the nature of an

unknown material by a thorough and complete analysis of everything contained in it. He employs painstaking and meticulously accurate methods of analysis and he depends upon chemical laws ("natural" laws) which have given him adequate grounds for concluding that certain reagents produce invariable reactions and results that are identical under comparable conditions. In other words, he depends upon his experimental evidence to inform him of the nature and content of the material under investigation.

Dr. Brown's methods of examining the content of the Bible remind me strongly of the technique of the chemical laboratory. He bases his opinion of the Bible in part upon his experimental evidence of the nature of its content. When, like an analytical chemist, he has determined the content, he turns to the clinical evidence of the way this powerful reagent reacts upon human lives. He points out that he finds God's Word a remedy for every sort of spiritual ill:—it is a tonic to correct the spiritual anemia growing out of spiritual malnutrition; it is an agent for cleansing and purifying the heart and life; in brief, it is unlike every other book in the world; it wonderfully heals the wounds inflicted by a hostile and selfish world; it even corrects mental disorders and removes the blood lust from the heart of the killer.

As vitamines and hormones in their chemical and biochemical behaviour, catalyze and promote health and growth, so the marvellous Word of God promotes spiritual health and growth, for it is combined food and medicine for the spiritual man. The living Word carries the elements of spiritual life—and it has produced unique transformations in the lives of millions of men, altering both their habits of thought and habits of life. What we may by analogy call both the "critical analysis" and the "clinical evidence" agree; this is **God's** Word and it lives from age to age and continuously reacts with changeless power to purify and ennoble and transform sinful lives in a hundred generations of men. For it points the way by which the Holy Spirit makes a new creature in Christ Jesus—an accomplishment more wonderful than the transmutation of one chemical element into another of quite different properties as brought about in the laboratory of the atomic physicist. And if Christ lives, so shall they that are Christ's live also. God be praised!

CHARLES M. A. STINE,
Ph.D., Sc.D., LL.D.

CONTENTS

	Page
INTRODUCTION	
Footprints of God	15
CHAPTER ONE	
The Folly of Atheism	19
CHAPTER TWO	
Matter	35
CHAPTER THREE	
Life	53
CHAPTER FOUR	
The Starry Universe	77
CHAPTER FIVE	
The Earth and Life Conditions	93
CHAPTER SIX	
Water and Air	107
CHAPTER SEVEN	
Plant Life	145
CHAPTER EIGHT	
Animal Life	165
CHAPTER NINE	
The Human Body	221
CHAPTER TEN	
Seeing God	237

ERRATA

On page 86, line 10 from the top, where it states, "6 and twenty-four ciphers," it should read, "6 and twenty-one ciphers."—The Publishers.

INTRODUCTION

FOOTPRINTS OF GOD

Scientists finding fossil footprints of extinct dinosaurs assure us that these great creatures must have roamed the earth in the long ago. As they walked upon the semi-solid earth, gradually hardening into rock, they left these indisputable evidences of their existence.

God has trod this earth; He has travelled the infinite depths of space leaving His mark on everything touched. The starry heavens are studded with countless universes flung from His omnipotent hand. He has set them in their destined locations and marked out for them their appointed speeds and orbits.

"In the beginning God created," is the only satisfactory explanation of heavens and earth. Following the catastrophic destruction of the first beautiful and perfect creation, "the Spirit of God moved upon the face of the waters." Darkness gave way to light when those sublime words, "Let there be light," penetrated the stygian depths of absolute night. All the products of His infinite power and wisdom were pronounced "good."

The wonders of the firmament which He called "heaven" sprang instantly into being. Hills and mountains rose as valleys and oceans descended to their appointed places.

The miracle of grass, herb and fruit-tree appeared to cover the earth with a carpet of loveliness. Colors, rich, rare, and ravishing, were splashed over all—gorgeous hues of red, orange, yellow, blue, indigo, and violet,—the Master Artist of the universe at work!

His tender hands touched the delicate petals of flowers throughout the world when no one but God and the angels could see their beauty. On the canvas of the skies He painted the glorious tints of ever-changing sunsets, flinging across the dome of heaven a gigantic rainbow as His signature to the promise which guarantees to the world safety against future destruction by a flood of waters.

He set the sun, moon and stars where it

pleased Him in the fathomless heavens "to give light upon the earth, and to rule over the day and over the night, and to divide the light from the darkness."

From the depths of infinite Wisdom came all the varied forms of life, from the infinitesimal infusorium, up through strange myriads of insect life, winged birds, great sea-monsters, all the citizenry of the ocean depths. To the land He summoned cattle and creeping things, beasts of the earth small and great, all "after their kind."

"And God saw that it was good."

As we begin our study of these miraculous operations of Deity we seem to hear the words of God spoken to His servant Moses one ancient day at the base of Mt. Horeb when the flaming bush was ablaze with fire but was not burned: "Put off thy shoes from off thy feet for the place whereon thou standest is holy ground."

With reverent awe and holy exultation let us examine the footprints of God. As we venture into this "Holy of Holies" we shall get a vision of the invisible One. We shall appreciate the truth and the significance of the great words in Romans 1:20:

> "For the invisible things of Him since the creation of the world are clearly seen, being perceived through the things that are made, even His everlasting power and Deity; so that they are without excuse."

The reader will please note that Scripture Quotations throughout the book are taken from The American Revised Version.

CHAPTER ONE

THE FOLLY OF ATHEISM

The most characteristic feature of this sin-stricken world is its refusal to acknowledge God. This blasphemous attitude is not solely the prerogative of those self-styled atheists who blatantly and impudently deny the existence of any Supreme Being possessing Personality. It applies also, even if in lesser degree, to the rank and file of humanity. Judging from the abundantly available evidence at our disposal, the majority exhibit little inclination towards any real recognition of God, and comparatively few desire fellowship with Him.

Where can we find a nation that pays more than empty lip service to God? Confronted with the greatest crisis since the dawn of history and threatened with imminent destruction, our leaders occasionally mention the name of God in a hazy, indefinite, apologetic manner. It is a futile gesture reflecting a somewhat disturbing and almost submerged conviction that somewhere there may be a Supreme Being, and it might be well to offer this slight recognition of the fact that possibly God does exist.

What a surprising shock it would be if any government official occupying high office would have the courage to say a word in behalf of the "Lord Jesus Christ"!

About the only time the world mentions this holy name is in swearing and blasphemy. The only possible end to this defiant challenge to the Saviour of the world is judgment sure and terrible when God's wrath breaks on a Christ-rejecting universe.

The extent of the permeation of our higher institutions of learning with atheism is shown by Dr. James H. Leuba of Bryn Mawr College in his book, "Belief in God and Immortality," containing the results of a widespread questionnaire sent by him to hundreds of professors and an equally large number of students. His statistics are probably near to the truth and, if so, are tragically suggestive as to the elimination of God by these men and their students.

Of the great number of replies received he finds the following percentage of avowed atheists:

Psychologists	86%
Biologists	82%
Sociologists	81%
Historians	68%
Physicists	66%

He finds that between 40 per cent and 50 per cent of the students, on graduating, reject the idea of God. It is easy to understand this wreckage of faith after four years of teaching by men who make no secret of their atheism.

Because God cannot be seen by mortal vision men are prone to conclude that He does not exist. Certain sophisticated individuals proclaim vehemently that they will believe only what they can see. Lallande, the astronomer, once said: "I have swept the entire heavens with my telescope and I have found no God." Therefore, he argued, there is no such Being.

How foolish to draw any such inference

from the very limited evidence supplied by a telescope. God cannot be discovered by any such mechanical device, but the eye of faith will soon find Him.

The unbeliever depends trustfully on the scope and accuracy of his five senses. He attributes to them great powers. What they reveal he will accept; what they do not disclose he will reject.

One thing that strikes me forcibly is that the skeptic must have acquired a pronounced faith in the clarity of his intellect and in the infallibility of his senses. When we examine them, however, we discover their obvious limitations.

We have eyes — what do we see? The range of visible light is very narrow. Our eyes can run the gamut from the short waves of violet to the long waves of red. There are waves beyond violet and waves beyond red which are invisible to us—two infinite worlds of color above and below these points that are completely hidden from our gaze. Shall we dare to say they do not exist because we cannot seen them? Our sense of sight, then, is far from infallible.

There is sound. We have two ears to catch a little of it. The ear can hear vibrations as musical notes only between certain limits. A single vibration produces the sound of a tap or blow, and each vibration is heard as a separate tap or blow until 16 or more occur in every second of time. Then a continuous sound results, the vibrations of which are not separable to the sense of hearing.

The lowest note on the organ is usually produced by a pipe 16 feet long which gives 32 vibrations per second. This note is named C'''. An 8-foot pipe gives its octave with 64 vibrations — C''. The double octave C' has 128 vibrations in a second and so on.

The highest audible note is said to have about 40,000 vibrations a second but is too feeble to have any musical value. So we hear sounds produced by vibrations of 20 to 40,000 per second.

Beyond and at each end are vast worlds of silence. There are untold numbers of sound waves that our ears cannot detect despite megaphones and amplifiers. Our ears then are far from being infallible guides to sound waves.

The senses of touch, taste and smell have the same marked limitations, the existing faculties scarcely touching these vast shores.

Our minds cannot grasp the mysteries of time and space. We are totally unable to understand eternity—that, actually, time had no beginning and will have no ending. Our imagination staggers when we think of infinite and immeasurable space. If we are to find God with these senses of ours, we shall be doomed to failure.

There are other phases to this discussion. We are endowed with appetites and longings; we are hungry—there is food. We have the instinct to love—there are those to love. We are eager for power and wealth—they are to be had. For every single desire there is a possible fulfillment.

Put a potato plant in the dark cellar. It is born with the instinct that there is sunlight to be found and so there is. Accordingly the vine searches until it finds the rays from the sun — the rays necessary for its life and growth.

There is no savage tribe, no civilized race that has not searched for God and longed for immortality. It is the earliest, deepest and most passionate desire of mankind. All other desires and instincts have an answer. Will this innate consciousness and longing for God be forever denied? It is incredible.

This instinct, this emotion, this belief,—call it what you will—is more powerful than any other. It has conquered love, and even the fear of death. It has built civilizations. It has set the spires of churches in the valleys around the world.

If this be a fable it is a mighty tough one to kill. They wrote it off the books in the French Revolution, but it soon sneaked in at the back door. They liquidated it in Russia, but it is filtering in again. They buried it in the catacombs of Rome, but it escaped and soon covered the earth. They crucified it; it was born again, rising into newness of life and vigor, victorious over death and the grave.

In the crises of life men turn instinctively towards God. Last April Brigadier General William R. Arnold, chief of the chaplains of the Army of the United States, released a story from his voluminous files producing evidence of the reaction of a soldier to the screaming shadows of death falling from the skies. He tells the experience of Lieut.-Col. Warren Clear on Bataan.

The colonel, who was never a habitual churchgoer, leaped into a fox-hole in the midst of an intense bombardment from the air. A sergeant squeezed over to make room. When explosions opened the earth and ripped trees roundabout, the noncom prayed aloud without any shame. Words forgotten since childhood soon came to the officer's lips as he echoed his companion's beseechings for divine protection.

After the enemy planes had passed over, Clear remarked more to himself than to his companion: "We prayed!" "Yes," replied the other quite casually, "we did. There are no atheists in the fox-holes of Bataan."

This is but an echo of the statement in Psalm 14: "The fool hath said in his heart, There is no God." The fact of God is the basis of all logical thinking, the foundation of any rational conception of the origin of things, the only hope for individuals or nations in time or eternity. God is the only scientific and satisfying explanation of the universe and all things therein.

An infidel science boasts that it needs no God. In His place it places evolution, the greatest hoax ever foisted on a credulous world. The believer in Creation and God is held up to scorn and ridicule because he accepts the supernatural. The sophisticated scientific infidel professes to reject anything which savors of miracle and confidently appeals to Natural Law.

Will he then be good enough to explain to me how I can send an electric current through a copper wire at 60 degrees below zero, and at the other end of the wire, heat a platinum wire to thousands of degrees? Where was that heat? From whence did it come?

A storage battery weighing fifty pounds, fully charged, will do work in lifting 100 pounds until its "soul" has been discharged. Still the battery has lost none of its fifty pounds. Why and how?

There is no end to questions like these revealing that we are compelled to accept many things contrary to reason and Law as we understand it.

Actually however, an evolutionist proclaims his faith in the most amazing miracles and yet can suggest no power or method that could possibly perform them. We do believe in miracles and we have a miracle-working God. "He spake and it was done, He commanded and it stood fast."

That certain Laws operate in the universe is obvious. Behind the Law must be a Law-Giver. We observe plan and design everywhere requiring a designing Intelligence to bring them into action. To persist in affirming that no God is needed to account for the intricate and exact operations of Nature is to deny the irresistible logic of our reasoning faculties. A multitude of great scientists have thus been compelled to admit the existence of a Supreme Personality. There is no other adequate solution that will satisfy our mind's questioning.

Dr. Robert A. Millikan writes in "The Commentator," June, 1937:

> "Everyone who reflects at all believes ... in God. ... To me it is unthinkable that a real atheist should exist at all. ... If you, in your conception, identify God with Nature you must attribute to Him consciousness and personality, or better, superconsciousness and super-personality. You cannot possibly synthesize nature and leave out of it its most outstanding attributes. Nor can you get these potentialities out of nature no matter how far back you go in time. In other words, materialism as commonly understood is an altogether absurd and utterly irrational philosophy, and is so regarded, I believe, by most thoughtful men."

In "God and the Cosmos," Dr. Theodore Graebner quotes Prof. Shepardson, a noted electrical engineer of international fame as he writes in "The Religion of an Electrical Engineer":

> "The evidence obtainable from study of material phenomena gives us confidence in concluding that a Supreme Being exists, that He is profoundly intelligent, that He designed and constructed and governs the universe, and that He encourages those who seek to learn of His works and ways. ...

The scientist with a smattering of secondhand knowledge may presume to ridicule the simple statements of remarkable events, but the real scientist recognizes that what he does not know is far more than what he does know and his mind is on the alert for additional knowledge. . . . Jesus Christ was either the Son of God or else a deceiver, and the evidence all points to His being genuine."

Sir James Jeans, the eminent British astronomer, writes in "The Mysterious Universe" as follows:

"Our modern minds have, I think, a bias towards mechanical interpretations. Part may be due to our early scientific training; part perhaps to our seeing continually everyday objects behaving in a mechanical way; a mechanical explanation looks natural and is easily comprehended. Yet in a completely objective survey of the situation, the outstanding fact would seem to be that mechanics has already shot its bolt and has failed dismally, on both the scientific and philosophic side.

"Thirty years ago we thought or assumed that we were heading towards an ultimate reality of a mechanical kind. It seemed to consist of a fortuitous jumble of atoms, which was destined to perform meaningless dances for a time under the action of blind purposeless forces, and then fall back to form a dead world. Into this wholly mechanical world, through the play of the same blind forces, life had stumbled by accident. One tiny corner at least, and possibly several tiny corners of this universe of atoms had chanced to become conscious for a time, but were destined in the end, still under the action of blind mechanical forces, to be frozen out and again leave a lifeless world.

"Today there is a wide measure of agreement . . . that the stream of knowledge is heading towards a non-mechanical reality; the universe begins to look more like a great thought than like a great machine. . . .

"We discover that the universe shows evidence of a designing or controlling power that has something in common with our individual minds . . . the tendency to think in the way which, for want of a better word, we describe as mathematical. . . .

"We have already considered with disfavor the possibility of the universe having been planned by a biologist or an engineer; from the intrinsic evidence of His creation, the Great Architect of the Universe now begins to appear as a Pure Mathematician."

Lord Kelvin, one of the greatest if not ac-

tually the greatest physicist of all time and at the time of his death acclaimed the most notable scientific genius in the world, says in "Christian Apologetics," p. 25:

> "I cannot admit that with regard to the origin of life science neither affirms nor denies creative power. Science positively affirms creative power, which it compels us to accept as an article of faith....We are absolutely forced by science to believe with perfect confidence in a Directive Power,—in an influence other than physical, or dynamical, or electrical forces."

Many expressions of opinion along these lines could be given from a host of great scientists. It is satisfying indeed to listen to such a galaxy of first magnitude stars in the scientific firmament speaking with unshaken conviction regarding their belief in God. We are in good company when we exclaim with Job: "I know that my Redeemer liveth."

One does not need to be a scientist to arrive at the same conclusion. Plain common sense compels us to form the same judgment. A few years ago the American Magazine published a business man's statement of the reason for his belief in God. This man wrote:

"It takes a girl in our factory about two days to learn how to put the 17 parts of a meat chopper together. It may be that these millions of worlds each with its separate orbit, all balanced so wonderfully in space—it may be that they just happened; it may be that by a billion of years of tumbling about they finally arranged themselves. I don't know. I am merely a plain manufacturer of cutlery. But this I do know, that you can shake the 17 parts of a meat chopper around in a washtub for the next 17 billion years and you'll never have a meat chopper."

Anyone who studies the wonders of the stars and planets with their astonishing system and order will come to the same faith. The great Sir Isaac Newton, one of the greatest minds of all time, spoke with authority on this point when he said:

"This admirably beautiful structure of sun, planets and comets could not have originated except in the wisdom and sovereignty of an intelligent and powerful Being. From a blind metaphysical necessity, which, of course, is the same always and everywhere, no variety could originate. The whole diversity of created things, in regard to places and times, could have had its origin only in the ideas and will of a necessarily existing Being."

CHAPTER TWO

MATTER

There are 92 elements which constitute all kinds of matter, from Hydrogen at one end of the scale to Uranium at the other. Matter is formed from particles known as molecules which are a combination of atoms. Inside the atoms science affirms there are infinitely minute particles called electrons, thought to be charges of negative electricity. Each atom also is said to contain at least one proton which is a charge of positive electricity. Other curious and infinitely small particles such as neutrons and positrons have also been discovered in the atom as science seeks to unravel the unfathomable mystery of matter.

Hydrogen, the first element in the table, is the extremely light, inflammable gas which the Germans used to fill their Zeppelins. It is one of the constituent parts of water and is found in many other substances. Its presence in fuels is usually revealed by the blue flame produced.

The atom of Hydrogen has, as far as science has been able to determine, only one positively charged particle, or proton, in its nucleus. Around this is the swiftly moving, negatively charged electron.

Though the two particles exactly counterbalance each other in electrical charge, the mass of the proton has been calculated as being 1845 times as great as the mass of the electron. Thus the proton accounts for practically the entire mass of the atom.

The nucleus of the atom may contain more than one proton. As we proceed upward from hydrogen in the table of elements we find more and more protons and even electrons squeezed into the relatively small nucleus. When we reach uranium the complexity of the atoms of the elements has greatly increased. In the atomic nucleus of uranium there are said to be 92 protons and 146 neutrons along with 92 out-revolving electrons.

In addition to the 92 elements there are many compounds—substances whose building blocks consist of combinations of atoms of various elements. Theodore L. Handrich writes interestingly in his book, "Every-Day Science" about them and every student of science gazes with astonishment at what he sees on examination of these mysterious substances.

The water molecule consists of two hydrogen atoms and one oxygen atom. These molecules, which are other fundamental units of matter, vary from the simplest, as those of water, to others containing thousands of atoms all combined in definite proportions and patterns. A crystalline protein molecule from the juice of diseased tobacco plants apparently consists of about 2,000,000 atoms. A slight change in the proportion of one element to another in a molecule can alter the compound so radically that it has entirely different properties.

Between hydrogen and uranium lie all the other elements with many differing combinations, each obeying some rigid law which governs its operations. There must be an infinite Mind behind the origin of matter to bring into being these infinitesimal particles, and then cause them to combine in innumerable ways according to some prearranged plan. Will any such terms as Struggle for Existence or Survival of the Fittest suffice as an explanation of their existence? Could these lifeless particles possibly create themselves? The question answers itself.

While the 92 kinds of atoms are distinct and separate those of each particular form are absolutely similar in structure and performance. As Graebner says: "They are like coins struck in a mint each bearing the impress of the image of their maker in the attributes they possess."

Another wonderful feature of atoms is that while those of the same element are alike in size, shape, weight, and other properties, the electrons in all the elements are identical as to their properties. This suggests the ultimate identity of all the elements in the constitution of all matter. Different kinds of matter, therefore, would differ only in having different numbers of electrons with different velocities within or around their fields of positive electrification or around their positive nuclei.

And if the proton portion of the atom consists of granular particles, then these particles, like the electrons, must also be the same for all the so-called chemical elements. In other words, all matter would be composed of the same electrons, protons, deutrons, positrons, neutrons, differing only in their numbers, arrangements and revolutions.

Is the human mind able to contemplate anything more amazing than this? Such a conception and the power to make it work belong only to Deity.

The chemical laws which compel these elements to combine according to atomic weights, and the law of multiple proportions, show the infinite wisdom of the Creator. Each atom of matter is stamped with laws that are definite and invariable so that it acts with absolute precision in all that it does. 32 pounds of sulphur must have 56 pounds of iron with which to unite, no more, no less, and so with all the elements.

In these various chemical compounds are found molecules of varying complexity with atoms of increasing number. From water with its three atoms, Nitric Acid with five, Caffeine with 24, Quinine with 48, we pass on up to the mysterious Protein molecule with hundreds and thousands of atoms, a formation which staggers the imagination.

L. J. Henderson writes in "The Order of Nature," p. 201:

> "The properties of elements are to be regarded as fully determined from the earliest conceivable epoch, and perfectly changeless in time."

J. E. Boodin, in "Cosmic Evolution," p. 21, refers to the same wonder:

> "Spectral analysis identifies the presence of the same elements with the same properties in other parts of the cosmos and that seems to hold irrespective of the age and temperature of the celestial bodies. We know that meteoric iron has the same specific gravity and properties as terrestrial iron. In the absence of evidence to the contrary we may then regard the properties of elements as constant."

L. Franklin Gruber, writing in "Whence Came the Universe," remarks:

> "What skill or intelligence must be necessary to build up such complex infinitesimal

structures in their countless duplicates, all exactly alike for the same substance. Yet so wonderful are the workings of nature's mysterious laboratory that no two of the same kind among the countless number of these molecules, wherever found throughout nature, differ in the least detail. Surely a law is operative here that requires an infinitely intelligent Law-Giver."

Fifty years ago, the great scientist Clerk-Maxwell delivered a lecture before the British Association for the Advancement of Science in which he said:

"None of the processes of Nature since the time when Nature began, have produced the slightest difference in the properties of any molecule. On the other hand, the exact equality of each molecule to all others of the same kind, gives it, as Sir John Herschel has well said, the essential character of a manufactured article, and precludes the idea of its being eternal and self-existent. Science is incompetent to reason upon the creation of matter itself out of nothing. We have reached the utmost of our thinking faculties when we have admitted that because matter cannot be eternal and self-existent, it must have been created."

Modern utilization of the astonishing powers of these elements, and their ability to combine in various ways and to undergo slight changes resulting in the appearance of new substances, reads like a chapter from the Arabian Nights. It is a fairy tale come true as the twentieth-century chemist rubs his "Aladdin's lamp" and watches the new products of his genius spring into existence.

One of the most interesting and authoritative surveys of these chemical developments was given recently by one of the world's leading chemists. Dr. Charles M. A. Stine, chief chemist of E. I. du Pont de Nemours & Co., and Vice President of the same company, addressed the American Chemical Society at Buffalo, N. Y., on September 7th.* He referred to the certain accomplishments of chemistry in the near future. All these incredible prospects are made possible because of the divinely-conferred properties of matter. He said:

> "When we, the American people, on the seventh day of December, 1941, found ourselves again at war on a global scale, we were living on a plane that bore but little

---
*Chemical and Engineering News, Sept. 10, 1942.

resemblance to the pre-war period of a quarter-century earlier. Our clothes, our foods, our homes were different. . . .

"Hosiery and furniture alike were being made from coal, water and air; dresses from wood, farm fertilizers from the atmosphere, camphor from pine stumps. These and many other achievements of chemical synthesis had altered or made obsolete trade practices and customs as old as the race. . . . The scientist was just getting started. Tens of thousands of new chemical compounds and metallic alloys awaited his full exploration. We were speculating on the eventual conquest of disease. The elimination of poverty, at least as a social problem, was considered as a goal that well might be realized. And as organic chemistry was the source-spring of a major share of the infinitude of changes that inspired such hopes, the influences of the First World War could be definitely traced here also. Our organic chemical industry grew directly in answer to needs violently made evident by that war. . . .

"The chemical synthesis of vitamins, to say nothing of hormones and sulfa drugs, not only is revolutionizing medicine and dietetics but putting these sciences on incomparably higher planes of performance and future promise. . . .

"Already our world of 1940, in which we took such pardonable if mistaken pride, is so distant in the past that it has become an antiquity when seen through scientific eyes. The inconceivables of two years ago are today's realities.

"More than a century was consumed in bringing the crude rubber production of the world up to a million tons yearly. Now in less than two years, the United States alone is undertaking to accomplish as mighty a feat, by the manufacture of chemical rubbers from petroleum, alcohol, coal and limestone.

"By the end of 1943, our production of aluminum will be at a rate almost seven times greater than was attained in 1939 after 50 years of intensive development. And we will be recovering from brine, sea water, and other sources approximately 100 times the amount of magnesium that was produced in 1939, when the magnesium industry was 24 years old. . . .

"Largely as a result of chemical advances in fuels, plastics and light metals, air-craft engineers are designing transoceanic planes capable of flying to Europe and back, non-stop, carrying payloads of 20 tons.

"The projected planes are quadruple the size of the famous "Clipper" planes that pioneered in inaugurating trans-Atlantic commercial service.

"The nation will emerge from this war with capacities for making plastics, synthetic fibres, nitrates, hydrocarbons, high octane gasolines and literally scores of chemical and other raw materials on a scale that only two years ago was beyond our comprehension. . . .

"The aluminum-producing capacity being created will furnish in one year metal enough to build thrice the number of passenger cars now operating on all American railroads. To produce this aluminum will require more electricity annually than was consumed in 1940 in 27 of our 48 states. . . . Aluminum has become a major metal.

"Magnesium is about 60% the weight of aluminum and about one-fifth the weight of steel. . . . Half a ton of magnesium, on the average, is going into every American fighting plane that is built. . . .

"Very significant is the source of most of the magnesium now employed industrially. For the first time in history a structural metal is being obtained from the sea by a chemical process. Huge pumps force 300,000,000 gallons of sea water daily through intricate apparatus. At present, magnesium and bromine are the only products precipitated but potentially the water contains traces of every element found on land. Are we opening a new field in chemistry far more bizarre than any of the imaginings of fictionists? Nobody knows as yet.

"Steel is challenging the lighter metals. Low alloy steels and new modifications of the higher alloy steels, fresh from the laboratory, are bidding for expanding uses in aviation and wherever lightness and strength are requisites. In the steel industry today technicians speak confidently of monster air-craft that will be largely steel. These new alloys are three times the weight of aluminum and almost five times the weight of magnesium, but their tensile strength approximates 190,000 pounds to the square inch. . . .

"Watch petroleum. Some years ago it was believed that the ultimate in motor fuel would be reached by the creation of a gasoline equivalent in power and anti-knock qualities to pure iso-octane. So superior was iso-octane that it was given an octane number of 100 which became the standard in evaluating all gasolines. But that was before the Battle of Britain. . . .

"Now fuels can be made that go beyond the octane scale. . . . They deliver one-half again as much power as 100 octane fuel. . . . The petroleum chemist now sees all existing motors as out of date, with knowledge of fuels advancing so rapidly that September's motor might be out of date in October....

"A barrel of crude oil contains literally thousands of chemical compounds ... almost anything under the sun might be created with these chemical building blocks of hydrogen and carbon; by the addition of oxygen and other elements in proper combination, he may obtain new alcohols, esters, acids, solvents, perfumes, pharmaceuticals and organic synthetics of every type, catalytic cracking processes and adaptations of them . ... are now leading toward this goal and taking petroleum chemistry into a realm once exclusive to coal-tar chemistry. . . . The catalytic cracking capacity of American oil companies will soon be hundreds of thousands of barrels daily. The significance of this development is beyond all present vision. . . .

"Synthetic rubber, which ... is not rubber at all but a new material of broader and yet more promising utility, is being produced from butadiene and styrene synthesized from petroleum. Toluene, best known as the basis of one of the most important of modern high explosives but also essential in dye chemistry and many other industries, is now a petroleum product.

> "With almost equal facility the petroleum chemist can give us ethylene on the one hand, or benzene on the other. . . . This feat might be likened to drawing wine or water at will from the same cask, or getting beef or pork from the same animal. . . . Ethylene and benzene are members of quite different chemical families . . . they are employed in the manufacture of plastics, synthetic rubbers, drugs, dyes, and nylon."

This long quotation from a remarkable address has been given because in a striking manner it corroborates what has been written in regard to the absolute necessity of a Supreme Intelligence planning and incorporating wonderful powers in these elements which when viewed superficially give no promise of their miraculous possibilities.

Dr. Stine indulges in a prophetic pronouncement of coming marvels which may well close this chapter. If these things mentioned by him become facts—and he speaks with knowledge and authority—it would appear that we are nearing millennial days.

Peering into the near future, Dr. Stine says:

> "The newest and most versatile of plas-

tics will be available after this war on a scale beyond all previous conceptions. The high-pressure synthesis of ammonia, one of the major chemical exploits of the century, will have taken on an industrial status that, in terms of producing capacity, may be comparable to the discovery of a sixth continent. The amount of fertilizer chemicals that this new capacity will be able to supply farmers will be so large that basic trends of agriculture might be changed. And these comprise but one group of a hundred or more products stemming from this high-pressure synthesis, which utilizes air, water, and coal as its building blocks.

"We will have glass that is unbreakable and glass that will float, wood that will not burn, and laminations of plastics and wood that will compete with structural metals. Hosiery derived from the air, water and coal, a wonder of pre-war days, is but the forerunner of many innovations from the same source, ranging from shoes that contain no leather and window screens that contain no wire, to machinery bearings that contain no metal.

"Fuels and metals and plastics will complete the revolution in transportation begun early in the century. . . . New cars will be of incredible efficiency. . . . The new models now gathering dust in dealers' storerooms have aged, technically, at least two decades. We are now in the 1960's of motor cars. . . .

"Sealed cooling systems . . . may end the nuisance of adding water to radiators. Weights may be half what they are, saving from 1500 to 2000 pounds of useless load. The power output per cubic inch of piston displacement may double, treble and even quadruple. Fuels may yield 50 miles to the gallon or more . . . fuels with octane ratings of 150 . . . gasoline may be displaced by a superior petroleum product . . . midget automobiles for children.

"Instead of rubber alone there will be a hundred and one rubbers for tires and other uses. . . . In aviation, hemisphere-spanning freighters . . . passenger air-carriers in fleets numbering hundreds of planes, trans-continental air-trains, nonstop gliders, which will drop off or pick up 'coaches' . . . wide popular use of small highly efficient, almost fool-proof planes at low cost.

"Houses from prefabricated sections, costing from $500 to $800 per room, sections so light that they can be handled by two men easily . . . new insulating materials, making possible light walls . . . plywood, plastics, rustless steels, non-ferrous alloys, fire-resistant woods . . . automatic lighting, governed by electric 'eyes' . . . air-conditioning units which filter out the pollens of hay-fever and asthma."

This notable paper written by a great scientist who is a sincere Christian believing in the God of the Bible will merit careful study. The new weapons which scientists are using to delve into the unknown mysteries of matter are themselves almost as unique as the facts they uncover. These include, as Dr. Stine points out, the ultra-centrifuge, in which there is a peripheral speed of the rotating disc comparable to the velocity of a rifle bullet. Still another is the electron miscroscope, expected to magnify 150,000 times. And there is the giant cyclotron or atom-smasher with which it is possible to transform certain ordinary elements into wholly different elements possessing radio-activity.

Anyone who can read these sentences revealing what God has made possible, and still refuse to accept the inevitable conclusion that there is an omnipotent and omniscient Creator, shows either hopeless bias or crass ignorance. As Dr. Stine remarked in this address: "Blessed is the nation whose God is the Lord."

CHAPTER THREE

LIFE

There are only two explanations that have ever been offered to account for life on this planet—spontaneous generation and creation. The first postulates an accidental combination of some of the lifeless particles discussed in the preceding chapter. They are supposed to have come together in such a way that life just "happened." The second gives the credit to God.

Because of its inherent absurdities and manifest impossibilities, spontaneous generation has been abandoned by almost every scientific authority of modern times. And yet Hendrik Van Loon, the well-known historian, writing in the widely read "Story of Mankind," permits the following nonsense to appear in the first chapter of his book, as he endeavors to give in simple language the weird evolutionary explanation of the first living cell and its descendants:

"In the beginning the planet upon which we live was, as far as we know, a large ball of flaming matter. After millions of years the surface burned itself out and was covered with a thin layer of rocks. Upon these lifeless rocks the rain descended in endless torrents. Finally the sun broke through the clouds. Then one day the wonder happened. What had been dead gave birth to life. The first living cell floated upon the waters of the sea. For millions of years it drifted aimlessly with the currents. During all this time it was developing certain habits that it might survive more easily upon the inhospitable earth. Some of these cells were happiest in the dark depths of the lakes and the pools. Others preferred to move about and they grew strange jointed legs. Still others depended on swimming in search of food, and gradually they populated the ocean. Some of the fishes left the sea and learned how to breathe. . . .

"Some of the reptilian family began to live in the tops of trees. They didn't need their legs for the purpose of walking about, but to move quickly from one branch to another, and they changed a part of their skin into a sort of a parachute which stretched between the sides

FOOTPRINTS OF GOD 55

of their bodies and the small toes of their feet.

"Gradually they covered the skin parachute with feathers and made their tails into a steering gear, and went from tree to tree and developed into true birds. The descendants of the reptiles became mammals by evoluting milk in a mother's breast, and dispensing with scales of fish and feathers of birds, covered their bodies with hair.

"One mammal in particular seems to surpass all others in its ability to find food and shelter. It had learned to use its forefeet for the purpose of holding its prey, and by dint of practice had developed a hand-like claw. This creature, half ape and half monkey, is supposed to have become the most successful hunter. . . ."

And this is the best that evolution can do in its frantic effort to bring man on the stage of the world from this first imaginary cell! Was there ever such a monstrous perversion of the facts of the case, teeming with fantastic and wholly imaginary and absolutely impossible changes throughout the alleged stages of evolutionary transformation?

This book is read in schools and colleges everywhere and is accepted as authoritative scientific statement. The Arabian Nights or Grimm's Fairy Tales can produce nothing more delightful than this product of a superheated imagination. Let us look at it.

Starting with the same words as Genesis but hardly with the same authority, we are solemnly informed that in the beginning our world was a "large ball of flaming matter." One wonders if this writer accepts the Nebular Hypothesis as these words might indicate. That explanation has universally been discarded but we pass on and note that fires were difficult to extinguish since they burned for "millions of years,"—all the inflammable material having been consumed, leaving just a layer of rocks on the surface. Then rain in endless torrents deluged the earth but one day the clouds cleared away and Old Sol broke through.

Now we are coming to the climax of events up to this time. There is water and heat and matter and as evolution MUST bring life somehow—this author dispenses with anything so unnecessary as an adequate Cause, and says that a great wonder happened. Note the latter word suggesting nothing of plan or design but simply and solely chance. "What had been dead gave birth to life."

This surely is the wonder of wonders—it never occurred before and never since, in spite of all the efforts of skeptical science to duplicate the performance. Countless thousands of experiments have been tried but each has signally failed. Without a scintilla of evidence to support this we are asked to surrender our belief in an omnipotent Life-Giver and take in its place this conglomeration of grotesque absurdity. As a matter of fact this atheistic concept is repudiated by practically every scientist of note who is willing to express himself on the subject.

Then see what happened to this earliest ancestor of the human race. He floated alone for millions of years upon the sea, drifting aimlessly with the currents. Poor, tiny, lonesome Granddaddy! But what a fighter he was according to this tale. He was a super-Methuselah—living not a thousand years, but MILLIONS,—yes millions, and during all this time planning to move out on land, and knowing that everything would be against him on the "inhospitable earth,"—he worked hard and long developing "habits" which would put him among the "fittest" who would survive. Van Loon does not mention any friends or relatives who might have relieved the loneliness of our progenitor, but suddenly we are told of other cells, who were happiest in the dark depths of lake and pool. Whence did they come, may we ask? And how? Granddaddy originally seems to have been alone and we are just wondering about this predicament which faces the author of this episode if he is to be able to make out a fair case. Did the first cell have the power of reproducing? Impossible, for we are told that for millions of years he—alone and unaided—drifted aimlessly with the currents. What longevity!—some cell—but it should be spelled—"SELL."

From primordial cell without a backbone, to worm,—still in the invertebrate class, first round, then long, and then one day another great wonder, a worm grows himself a backbone, and we have fish. This is said to be about twenty million years ago. "Man became a fish," wrote Dr. George Dorsey. It is hard to believe it. Our limited understandings are unable to grasp the wonders and intricacies of this evolving process. Any proof of these changes?—not the slightest!

Some of the fishes leave their watery habitat and the miracle continues. They do not die but "learn" how to breathe in air. Those who have extracted fish from water have always seen them die in short order, but this phenomenal evolutionary fish (this is a fish story, you know!) transformed himself into a frog, becoming the first amphibian in history, able to live under water or to breathe the atmosphere on land. From amphibians to reptiles is an easy transition for the evolutionary imagination, and we have become reptiles, taking up our residence "in the tops of trees." We are getting on!

The reptiles invent themselves a skin parachute, having advanced knowledge of areonautics, and float for short distances with this somewhat cumbersome device. But remember they were just learning—and how! The reptilian inventors brought all their powers to bear on the subject and came up with the feather idea, altering in some miraculous way the heavy scales into feathers, thus lightening the parachute with a tremendous improvement in transportation facilities.

A feather today is one of God's masterpieces wholly beyond the ability of mere man to duplicate but was not too difficult for the inventive reptilian geniuses.

But why follow this impossible account of mythical imaginings? One feels like apologizing for spending this much space on it and yet this is supposed to be up-to-date science and is being taught in schools everywhere. This writer from whom we have quoted seems to believe in spontaneous generation of life with all its vagaries and then follows it up by enumerating a host of ideas just as hopelessly impossible.

Of course one who rejects chance generation of life must of necessity accept its supernatural origin which is a hated concept by infidel science. Ernst Haeckel, the atheist, once fulminated in this way about it:

> "If we deny spontaneous generation there is no alternative except the unspeakable blasphemy implied in superstitious

FOOTPRINTS OF GOD 61

terms like 'miracle,' 'creation' and 'supernatural.'"

There is consensus of scientific opinion today that no form of life arises except from pre-existing life—"omne vivum ex vivo." Of the origin of organic life from inorganic material there is not an atom of proof. If the structure of lifeless matter cannot be accounted for without a Supreme Being, how much less possibility there is of explaining the infinitely complex operations of living things, without a God.

Biologists have tried ceaselessly to produce living protoplasm from non-living substances. All attempts have signally failed as we would expect them to fail knowing something of the wonders of this amazing material.

The following elements enter into the composition of all living bodies,—Carbon, Hydrogen, Oxygen, Nitrogen, Sulphur, Phosphorus, Chlorine, Potassium, Sodium, Calcium, Magnesium, Iron, with small amounts of Fluorine and Iodine in some,—fourteen in all.

A living cell is made up of many atoms of Carbon, Hydrogen, Oxygen and Nitrogen, with a small number of atoms of Sulphur and Phosphorus. The diameter of the living molecule is about one five-millionth of an inch, so that a speck of protoplasm one ten-thousandth of an inch in diameter would require not less than 500 of such molecules in a row to span it, and there would be no less than 125,000,000 of such molecules in the mass. To hope to create a bacillus would be as absurd as to expect to be able to manufacture a human body.

A brief glance at the wonders of protoplasm will show the absurdity of holding that once upon a time a fortuitous concourse of atoms was the accidental cause of this greatest of all mysteries.

Living matter shows four distinct phenomena:

1. Irritability—the property of responding in a particular way to the application of a stimulus.

2. Metabolism—the chemical changes produced as food materials are built up into higher forms and complex molecules already built up are broken down and their

effete products are excreted.
3. Growth—an increase in the size of the particular body until it reaches its destined form.
4. Reproduction — the process by which each living body insures the continuation of itself through its descendants.

These four processes constitute the operations of these microscopic bits of protoplasm called cells from which various other tissues are ultimately formed by a series of complex and exact changes which are impossible to understand so great is their intricacy. Each bit of living tissue seems to take its place in the line-up as if under the strictest orders from General Headquarters, G. H. Q.

The internal structure of these protoplasmic units reveals a thickened central portion known as the nucleus, surrounded by food material known as cytoplasm. In this latter there may be pigment granules, fat globules, glycogen particles, and spaces containing fluid. The most important part of the cell consists of chromatin threads which are to form into the miraculous chromosomes, the basis of all the changing forms of life. And all this in a tiny particle of tissue only about one one hundred and twenty-fifth of an inch in diameter. If you would like to know how large that is, sharpen a lead pencil to a fine point, press it gently on a piece of paper, and there you are! That is our size as we begin to develop.

The manner in which these cells divide and re-divide into countless thousands and millions, separating themselves into various groups to form the different tissues and organs, is an astounding miracle of miracles.

We have mentioned chromatin threads, the basis of the chromosomes. A brief study of these living forms will bring us face to face with God.

Each of us is a complex being different from every other person of the past or future. No two blades of grass are exact duplicates; neither are any two minds or bodies. Nature varies inheritance with a mathematical precision which prevents the exact duplication of any organ.

Nearly all living things begin with the fusing of two sex-cells, one from the male and the other from the female. This is fertilization, whereupon development begins. The single fertilized cell thus formed divides into two cells, these into four, the four into eight, and so on, until in time, there are millions of cells organized into the complete unit, plant or animal as the case may be.

These processes form a complicated chain, but they go forward with miraculous precision to the predestined end; in so doing they give rise to innumerable questions. If all living things are thus formed, why are they not all alike? Why, for example, is John Doe six feet tall, blue-eyed, with straight blond hair, while his brother Jim is a bare five feet five, with dark eyes and curly hair?

Why do trees have roots and trunks and limbs? Why do fish have fins instead of hands? Why do mules have long ears and practically no power of reproduction? The fascinating answer to all these questions is in one small word—genes.

The scientific definition of a gene is "a minute organic particle, capable of reproduction, located in a chromosome and responsible for the transmission of an hereditary characteristic." This definition contains only statements of fact for which there is sufficient experimental evidence to prove them beyond reasonable doubt.

To understand this definition we must begin with a description of cells. Cells, then, are no more uniform in structure than automobiles. They range in size from those of the bacteria which are on the very limit of microscopic visibility, to nerve cells several feet in length; in volume they range from an infinitesimal nothing to that of an ostrich egg. Nevertheless, they are all alike in many respects. All living cells are filled with water, and moving through this water is the substance called protoplasm. As we have seen above, in this protoplasm is a denser spot known as the nucleus. Until a cell is ready to split in two, the nucleus is a tangle of chromatin threads. As the cells prepare to split, the threads shorten and thicken, forming segments whose number is characteristic of the kind of cell—in man, the number is 48. These rod-like segments are the chromosomes and are made up of strings of genes. If we think of a string of beads, we may get a clearer idea,— the entire string standing for the chromosome and the individual beads for the separate genes.

In the last few years, the ultra-microscope and X-rays have given us a much better insight into what these genes are and how they perform their intricate operations. The evidence indicates that they are single complex protein molecules; that they reproduce by "growing" a new gene inside the old one, rather than by splitting in two; that in the chromosome they form strings held together by some unknown force; and that the order of the genes in these strings determines the characteristics of the particular cell containing them. In size they range up to 6 or 7 millionths of a centimeter in diameter.

In higher orders of life, there are thousands of these genes present in each cell, strung out like beads. Changes, called mutations, occur when these strings "cross over" and interchange some of their genes. From these changes result white races or black; geniuses or dolts; men or women.

If mutations occurred at random, we might

expect extreme changes in an organism from generation to generation, instead of the general similarities which carry through. Then, evolution would be possible, but an omnipotent power has willed otherwise. Mice give birth to mice, and human beings reproduce human beings because of this inherent nature of their respective chromosomes. They work according to an absolutely inviolable law. Where and how did this law originate unless from a Supreme Law-Giver?

When chromosomes get together and trade genes, they deal only with those chromosomes which are similar to themselves. For instance and as a crude illustration, let us imagine a community made up of French, Swedes, English, etc., each of whom has several commodities to barter. But French will exchange only with French, Swedes with Swedes, and so on. It will easily be seen that the distribution of wealth in the community will be changed much less under these conditions than if all the residents got together and traded indiscriminately.

Similarly the chromosomes in a nucleus discriminate in favor of their own type, and thus the exchange of genes is not a random thing but is controlled to such an extent that like produces like. It is not hard for a Bible believer to understand this for ten times over in the first chapter of Genesis we read the words, "after its kind." How did Moses know so much about the mysterious laws of genetics in that far-off day unless divinely inspired?

When a cell splits, the chromosomes also split along their length, and each cell then receives its full complement of these priceless genes, presence of which is essential to continuity of life, of organization, of species.

But if each cell has its full allotment of genes, one would think that the number must double each generation, when the two sex-cells combine into one. In a remarkable way, this is prevented. When cells which are to become sex-cells split away from their parent-cells, they are automatically endowed with only half the usual number of chromosomes. It is as if some omnipotent Power says to a forming sex-cell: "Wait. When you grow up you will be a sex-cell—take only half as many chromosomes—you are going to find a mate with an equal number and everything will be right."

Is it possible for anyone familiar with these wonders not to believe in a personal, designing, omnipotent and omniscient God?

So, we see that life is far more than a mere mechanical process. The body of an organism is much more than a machine. This is just as true of a plant as of an animal. Dr. D. H. Scott, eminent British botanist wrote in "Extinct Plants and Problems of Evolution," p. 225:

> "The leaves are a mechanism; the stem is a mechanism; and so is the plant as a whole. But the general design and scheme of the machine was laid down once for all years ago and have never been departed from."

Who, it is pertinent to ask, laid down the plan? The answer again is GOD. This unchanging purpose runs through the entire system of plant life.

No one knows what this life principle is—it cannot be examined and science is completely in the dark as to its nature. We see how it works but its real character eludes all efforts to discover it.

As Dr. Alfred Russell Wallace wrote thirty years ago in "The World of Life," p. 3, so is the mystery today:

> "So marvellous and so varied are the phenomena presented by living things, so completely do their powers transcend those of all other forms of matter subjected to mechanical, physical, or chemical laws, that biologists have vainly endeavored to find out what is at the bottom of their strange manifestations, and to give precise definitions, in terms of physical science, of what 'life' really is."

Horatio Hackett Newman, geologist, wrote in "The Nature and Origin of the World and of Man," p. 52:

> "In all frankness it must be admitted that the problem of the origin of life has not been solved."

General Smuts, as quoted by Graebner in "God and the Cosmos," p. 129, said:

> "Recent astronomical theory has come to strengthen this view of life as an exceptional feature off the main track of the universe. For the origin of our planetary system is attributed to an unusual acci-

dent, and planets such as ours with a favorable chance for life are taken to be rare in the universe. Perhaps we may even say at the present epoch there is no other globe where life is at the level manifested on the earth."

He could more properly have said that life is unknown at all anywhere except on this globe.

James S. Haldane, distinguished physiologist, affirmed that

"The mechanistic speculations of the last century no longer afford any prospect of understanding life."

Professor Conn agrees in the following words:

"There is not the slightest evidence that living matter could arise from non-living matter. Spontaneous generation is universally given up."

And yet men like Hendrik van Loon and H. G. Wells will persist in the unscientific assertion that life came from dead matter sometime, somehow in the long ago. These denials of any such possibility could be multiplied indefinitely.

One more must suffice. Vernon Kellogg, ardent evolutionist of Stanford University, writing in "Evolution," again as quoted by Graebner, affirms:

> "Nobody has yet made an amoeba in a test tube, nor infusoria in a sterilized hay solution. Pasteur and Tyndall long ago exploded the naive claims of the believers in spontaneous generation. 'Omne vivum ex vivo.' It is only life that produces life. The amoeba-like bit of oil foam, with all of its realistic imitation of amoeba's movements, the most complex molecules created by the organic chemist, with all their identity of chemical elements with protoplasm, are all of that long way from amoeba and protoplasm which is measured and defined by the phrases, non-life and life. There is a great gulf between what is living and what is not. And that gulf creates the great question for evolutionists and non-evolutionists alike: the question of the origin of life."

We close this chapter with a quotation taken from Benson's splendid book, "Immensity," which everyone is advised to read. This statement is by Richard Bergman and appeared in the Moody Bible Institute Monthly:

> "No evolutionist can satisfactorily ex-

plain the origin of life, yet that alone is the foundation for knowledge as to the origin of species. Granted that life exists, marvelous things can be done with it in the air castles of the theorist. But with chagrin many otherwise anti-supernaturalists must borrow from theology in order to secure this footing. In desperation materialists have babbled about 'seeds of life from other planets,' and 'accidental chemical combination,' but such explanations prove only their ingenuity. A God who created a spark of life so potential that from it a world could unfold, certainly performed a miracle in so doing that is just as difficult to grasp by faith as is the Genesis account of the special creation of species. Only a fool would surrender his position in Genesis for such poor logic as is offered by modern speculations."

It seems to be wise in view of all the circumstances to continue to put our complete faith in the sublime statement of John 1:1-5.

"In the beginning was the Word and the Word was with God, and the Word was God. The same was in the beginning with God. All things were made through Him; and without Him was not anything made that was made. IN HIM WAS LIFE; and the life was the light of men. And the light shineth in the darkness; and the darkness comprehended it not."

CHAPTER FOUR

THE STARRY UNIVERSE

Many books on astronomy are available for the student—books such as Jeans' "The Mysterious Universe," or Benson's "Immensity."* This latter is highly recommended as an interesting and authoritative description of the heavenly wonders. Many of the facts mentioned herein are taken from Benson's volume.

Young's translation of the 19th Psalm brings us a message of supreme importance; in fact, it is God's opinion of the value and importance of this study:

"The heavens are recounting the honour of God, and the work of His hands the expanse is declaring.

Day unto day uttereth speech; And night unto night showeth knowledge.

There is no speech and there are no words. Their voice hath not been heard.

---
*Order from Fundamental Truth Publishers. Price $1.25.

(Yet) Into all the earth hath their line gone forth, And to the end of the world their sayings. For the sun he placed a tent in them,

And he (the sun), as a bridegroom, goeth out from his covering. He rejoiceth as a mighty one to run the path.

From the ends of the heavens is his going out; and his revolution is unto their ends, and nothing is hid from his heat."

And we read a few more passages,—Isaiah 40:25, 26; Job 38:31-33:

"To whom then will ye liken me, that I should be equal to him? saith the Holy One. Lift up your eyes on high and see: who hath created these? He that bringeth out their host by number; He calleth them all by name; by the greatness of His might, and because He is strong in power, not one is lacking."

"Canst thou bind the cluster of the Pleiades, or loose the bands of Orion?

Canst thou lead forth the Mazzaroth in their season? Or canst thou guide the Bear (Arcturus) with her train?

Knowest thou the ordinances of the heavens? Canst thou establish the dominion thereof in the earth?"

When we contemplate the grandeur and magnificence of the universes which surround

us we are compelled to recognize the power and wisdom of the Creator. Our tiny world which at times seems so large to our limited vision shrinks to nothingness—we become an infinitesimal atom in endless space.

Even a partial conception of the number, magnitude, and distance of the systems of worlds, infinite by every standard of measurement, along with the knowledge that these immense worlds have been spinning their way through the skies, at amazing and exact speeds, for ages maintaining their own meticulous orbits, brings us to the discovery that we are in the presence of omnipotent Deity. No other conclusion is possible.

Exultantly we exclaim with the Psalmist:

> "Great is the Lord and greatly to be praised; And His greatness is unsearchable.
>
> One generation shall laud Thy works to another, and shall declare Thy mighty acts.
>
> Of the glorious majesty of Thine honor, and of Thy wondrous works will I meditate. . . .
>
> He counteth the number of the stars; He calleth them all by their names.

Great is our Lord and mighty in power;
His understanding is infinite."
(Psa. 145:3-5; 147:4, 5.)

How many stars are there? Is it possible to give even an approximate calculation? The astronomers seem to be lost when they endeavor to tell us about this mighty host. The stars visible to the naked eye are comparatively few. Old Hipparchus who lived about 150 B. C., and was a noted astronomer of that day declared confidently that there were 1026 stars! Ptolemy followed him by a few years and corrected his predecessor affirming there are 1056—Ptolemy had missed all of 30.

The Bible declares repeatedly that it is not possible to number the stars. Until comparatively recent times this was considered to be nothing more than figurative language. In both celestial hemispheres the best eyesight will discover less than 5,000 stars, and when Jeremiah exclaimed in Jer. 33:22: "The host of heaven cannot be numbered," that, in the eyes of a critical science, was an egregious mistake.

Since January 7, 1610, when Galileo first

FOOTPRINTS OF GOD 81

viewed the heavens through a telescope, how tremendously has the number of stars been multiplied! The numbers grew from thousands to hundreds of thousands, to millions, to countless billions, when in 1920 the great 100-inch Hooker telescope was brought into action at Mt. Wilson Observatory.

Some have attempted the colossal task of taking a star census. The astronomers are sure now that there are, according to different calculations, from 100 to 270 billions of stars in our own galaxy. That this may be increased many times over when the 200-inch telescope is ready to peer into the far depths of space is more than probable.

Our own universe is but one of millions of others—how many millions or billions, no one can tell. Each of these is as large if not larger than ours, so we begin to see the hopelessness of the task of enumerating. This is what compelled Jeans to acknowledge: "All the universes between them must contain about as many stars as there are grains of sand on all the seashores of the world." Strange admission from a leader of modern science, paralleling the plain statements of Scripture.

And our God knows ALL their names! And His omnipotence confers on them the ability to leap through space at an incredible speed, and in exact orbits, since they are not lacking in power—His power.

The speed at which all worlds travel staggers the imagination. Our earth, for instance, is taking three trips simultaneously. We travel each year 9,000,000 miles at 1,000 miles an hour around our axis, a trip which is completed once every 24 hours; between 500 and 600 millions of miles at 19 miles a second around the sun; and lastly, we are traveling along with the sun at 13 miles a second, 400,000,000 miles a year as the entire solar system moves through its vast orbit which we are told requires millions of years to complete.

The human mind refuses to grasp these figures. They are beyond our understanding just as the great God who is able to give them these movements and maintain them, is infinitely beyond our understanding.

But the above speeds are slow when compared with the distance covered by the more distant universes,—100 miles a second to 15,000 miles in the same tick of the clock. Only light traveling at 186,300 miles a second exceeds the motion of these rapidly receding nebulae.

Benson writes in "Immensity," p. 100:

"So perfect is the movement of the earth around the sun and of the moon around the earth that astronomers know exactly when and where an eclipse took place thousands of years ago, and are equally sure of these facts concerning any eclipse that will take place in the future. . . . Why? Because of the inimitable precision of the movements of the heavenly bodies. . . .

"There are certain complications in the movements of the earth and moon that make their accuracy even more remarkable. . . . The path of the earth is not a circle, but an ellipse; that is, a circle flattened a little on two opposite sides. The result is that as we approach the flat parts of the circle, we draw nearer to the sun, and the powerful attraction of the latter accelerates the movement of the earth, until it can again get out of the sun's range. Yet in spite of this disturbance, and in spite of the fact that the earth is pulled three million miles nearer to the sun in January than in July, perfect time is maintained for the entire journey. If the speed is accelerated for a time, it is later reduced for the rest of the orbit, and the circuit is completed to the fraction of a second.

"In addition, the earth has to reckon with the moon, which is constantly at its heels with a tantalizing pull this way and that way, seemingly to tempt it away from its prescribed course and delay its journey. All these pulls of the moon do perturb the earth, as we can well judge from the effect we see on the ocean tides.

"Astronomers have to take into consideration these perturbations of the earth in charting its course, but strange to say, after allowance has been made for every side excursion, we still move on with inimitable precision. More than that. Both the earth and the moon have other movements besides that of their revolution— the latter no less than 60 distinct motions— yet with all these complications there is such perfect adjustment and harmony in every twist and turn that the sum total of all the deviations charts a constant course for these great bodies and carries them along on perfect time. What amazing forethought, wisdom and power are here displayed! All the intelligence and ingenuity of man could never construct so complicated a machine, or operate it by such perpetual and perfect movement."

Every star in the universe—and we have seen that their number is innumerable—has its own motion and orbit, which it maintains with the same exactness and precision.

Benson concludes his chapter on "Inimitable Precision," p. 108, with these lines which are well worthy of our meditation:

"Countless worlds are ever circling
Through the boundless realms of space,
And the God whose hand has made them
Keeps each orb in its true place.
All revolve in perfect order
Harmony complete we see,
Yet the God whose will they follow
Is the God who thinks of me."

What is to be said of the omnipotent Power of the Great God who can perform all these mighty wonders? We can understand the words of Job, as he thought of his God and extolled His majesty, chapter 26:13, 14:

"By His Spirit the heavens are made beautiful;
His hand hath pierced the swift serpent.
Lo, these are but the outskirts of His ways:

And how small a whisper do we hear of Him!
But the thunder of His power who can understand?"

We are more familiar with our tiny world than any other—so let us think of it again for a moment and its movements. Astronomers have calculated the weight of the globe as approximately 6,000 million, million, million tons—6 and twenty-four ciphers—an amount too great to imagine. A freight train with 100 heavily loaded cars must have one or two powerful engines to pull it slowly along the track. What shall we say of this Power, strong enough to carry an enormous load, evenly, easily, a mile every four seconds, at cannonball speed, without any creaking of the machinery, without boilers to generate steam, no dynamos to manufacture electricity, no visible machinery? If this is not God—what solution of the mystery can there be?

Whirling through space at this dizzy speed, why are not people by the thousand hurled off into space? The answer is gravitation, a power which exceeds the terrific centrifugal force of the earth's rotation, and is strong enough to reach out 238,000 miles and anchor the moon, so that it is compelled to remain in contact with the earth at this great distance.

The combined weight of all the worlds, all being moved at great speeds, is quite beyond the ability of the human intellect to compute. The vast distances of these universes from us are impossible to comprehend. Light travels at 186,000 miles a second and if the astronomers are right it takes 250,000,000 years for the light from some of these distant nebulae to reach our earth.

The only thing left for us is to cry with the Psalmist,—Ps. 104:24:

> "O Lord, how manifold are Thy works!
> In wisdom hast Thou made them all:
> The earth is full of Thy riches."

A moment's consideration of the size of the spheres which are hurtling through the heavens will be profitable. The Earth is a globe 8,000 miles in diameter and 25,000 miles in circumference, marvelous for its absolute spherical form and regularity, so that the mountains and ocean depths scarcely roughen the surface. "The varnish on a bowling ball would scarcely represent the surface irregularities of the Earth."

The earth is small but there are tinier planets —asteroids—some 1,265 having been discovered, most of them less than 100 miles in diameter. The other planets which make up our Solar system are well known—Mercury, Venus, Mars, Jupiter, Saturn, Uranus, Neptune and Pluto. Jupiter is the largest of all these, being 1,300 times the size of the earth. The sun is more than 1,300,000 times the size of the earth, being 866,000 miles in diameter.

But the sun, large as it is, is small compared with other worlds, all of the stars being distant suns and many of immense size. For instance, Betelguese, one of the stars in the constellation Orion, is 215,000,000 miles in diameter, 248 times as large as the sun.

Traveling from Betelguese to Antares, we are gazing at a gigantic world 400,000,000 miles in diameter, making even Betelguese look small. And yet we are told that there are remote suns inconceivably larger than any which have been mentioned.

Truly, "He doeth great things past finding out; yea, and wonders without number." (Job 9:9, 10.)

There is another arresting phase to this study. Not only are the motions of the heavenly bodies so exact that they form the standard of exact measurements for all human observations, but in the relation of the planets to each other, and their progressive distances from the sun—a fact first discovered by Titius of Wittenberg and brought to the attention of the scientific world by John Bode in 1772—there are evidences of design which exclude the notion of chance.

As Graebner puts it in "God and the Cosmos":

> "It is a remarkable fact that in the so-called Periodic Law of the elements constituting matter, the same relation is observed. Of the 92 elements no two have exactly the same capacity to resist heat, and no two atoms of the same elements have the same weight as compared with an atom of Hydrogen.
>
> "But these differences in resistance to heat and in weight, are not haphazard, but are so regularly progressive that they can

be arranged in a series of regularly increasing intervals. Most marvellous of all, however, when these differences in specific gravity are examined, we find they bear a close resemblance in their progressive distances from the sun. There appears to be one law for atoms and for worlds."

Edwin B. Frost of the Yerkes Observatory wrote in the Chicago Tribune, July 13, 1931, as quoted by Graebner, p. 69:

"We really don't know much after all. Everything that we learn from the observational point of view in the study of astronomy seems to me to point precisely and always toward a purposeful operation in nature.

"When you accept this, it seems to me to be inconsistent with physical sciences not to believe in a Mind behind the universe.

"I cannot imagine planets getting together and deciding under what law they should operate. Nor do we find anywhere in the solar or stellar systems the debris that would necessarily accumulate if the universe had been operating at random.

"The order that we do see does not appear to have been produced as the chance outcome of random motions coerced into some measure of uniformity. You cannot fail to recognize that law has been long at work when you examine the wonderful structure of the apirals. (He refers to the Andromeda nebula, the most gigantic spectacle in the universe.)

"In a purposeful creation I find it not at all inconsistent to believe that there must be a Mind developing the purpose. . . .

"We receive from this spiritual Power some gift, and we may develop it dimly and distantly after the model of the Creator's thought. If the universe is purposeful, then it is plain to me that man, who is the highest form of development on this earth, must himself be distinctly a result of purpose rather than accident."

These are powerful witnesses to the truth we are enunciating, that there must be a personal Creator. To reject this basic foundation of all human thought is not a sign of science and scholarship, but rather of ignorance and semi-knowledge. These men we have quoted are leaders in the scientific world and must be heard.

CHAPTER FIVE

THE EARTH AND LIFE CONDITIONS

That the earth is the only planet in the universe where life is possible, as we know it, is universally accepted today. Scientists have reluctantly arrived at this conclusion after examining carefully the conditions as to atmosphere, heat, water, etc., which obtain on every other world. There was a time when many articles were written to express the hope of life elsewhere than on this earth alone. Plans were considered for communicating with the people of Mars and the Sunday Magazine supplements of many papers described in exciting detail how this communication might be accomplished and the results.

But that day has gone. Now, the earth is definitely set apart because of the unique distinction that it alone possesses life conditions. That this could be due to chance would seem to be quite impossible.

Almost 40 years ago, Dr. Alfred Russel Wallace, the great scientist of the 19th century, wrote in that interesting book, "Man's Place in the Universe":

> "The earth is the only body capable of sustaining life. Life is not possible on any of the planets because they are either too close or too distant from the sun; some are probably composed of gas."

What, then, are the conditions necessary for life which are found exclusively on the earth? There are at least five. They may be enumerated as follows:

1. Regularity of heat supply.

2. Sufficiency of solar light and heat.

3. Abundance and general distribution of water.

4. An atmosphere of proper density and composition.

5. The length of day and night correctly adjusted to the requirements of humanity, as well as of vegetable and animal life.

Before we study these conditions there are a few general observations which ought to be made. These refer to the peculiar relation of the earth to other heavenly bodies, its size, its distance from the sun, the time it takes to revolve around the sun, and its strange elliptical orbit.

If it is true as asserted by scientists and as confirmed by the Bible, that in order to have life on any planet it must be of a certain size and weight, then we can understand something of the meaning of those sublime words in Job 38:4, 5 where God asks a direct question:

> "Where wast thou when I laid the foundations of the earth? Declare if thou hast understanding.
> Who determined the measures thereof, if thou knowest?"

The atmospheric mantle surrounding a planet is determined by the size and weight of the planet. This was one of the major points discussed by Wallace forty years ago and he concluded there was evidence of design in the size of our earth. He showed that if there was a difference, approximately, of only ten per cent either in decrease or increase, no life would be possible. The atmosphere would in the one case be too tenuous and in the other too dense.

The annual revolution of the earth around the sun, giving us the seasons, is interesting. We make the trip of 525,000,000 miles in 365 days, 5 hours, 48 minutes, and 46 seconds. If the earth lost five seconds in 1,000,000 miles, in 6,000 years there would be an error of more than six months with total disruption of the plan. But so exact is the timing that there is not more than one-thousandth of a second variation in a century. Midsummer and midwinter are as they were in the time of Adam and Noah.

The length of the year's orbit is exactly adapted to the requirements of plants and animals, or plants and animals are exactly adjusted to the length of the year. The vegetable clock is set to go for a year. During this time many things must happen. The juices must be formed, the sap raised, the leaves unfolded, the flowers expanded, the seed matured, the fruit ripened, and there must be time for rest and recuperation of the vital energies. The seasons as they exist give just the proper time for all these operations.

It is the same in the animal kingdom. The functions and energies and reproductive habits are adjusted to this yearly cycle. Birds are born, pair, build their nests, hatch out their young before the next winter comes; insects also. It surely looks like plan. And when we remember that the peculiar inclination of the earth's axis—$23\frac{1}{2}$ degrees from the perpendicular, causes the various seasons, we are convinced that a Supreme Designer is responsible. If the year were shortened three or four months there would be utter disorder and death everywhere.

Let us study the regularity and sufficiency of the light and heat supply for the earth. We shall find some startling facts. Here is a tiny bit of dust plunging through space where the cold is intense, separated by immense distances from its neighbors, carrying on its surface vegetable, animal and human life, all needing the most exact quantities of regular heat.

The 19th Psalm has already been quoted. Let us look at it again from the heat angle. This remarkable Psalm at one time was held up to ridicule because of its reference to the movement of the sun in a circular orbit of vast extent. It had been proved, apparently, by science that our sun was a fixed star without any proper motion of its own. The sun according to the Psalmist, hurries forth like an excited bridegroom and "rejoices as a mighty one to RUN his course."

No one today dares to speak slightingly of the science of the 19th Psalm. It is now accepted that the sun is not a fixed star without motion, but, as we have seen, is journeying on its way at the rate of thirteen miles a second, and furthermore, its circular orbit requires many millions of years to complete. The Psalm says that this trip takes the sun "from the ends of the heavens to the ends of the heavens." This is astonishing scientific truth especially when we remember that the Psalmist knew nothing of a telescope, and had no means of measuring star distances or movements. How did he get it right? God wrote the 19th Psalm!

The most interesting and suggestive statement about the sun is this: "Nothing is hid from the heat thereof." This certainly indicates the plan of God. The creatures He was to bring forth to dwell on the earth, must have, in order to live, certain very accurate provisions made for them. As mentioned, the first of these essentials is light and heat regularly and in just the right degree. The range of temperature within which life is possible is very narrow indeed. A comparatively few degrees either in the direction of cold or heat would result in death. So we note the delicacy of the balance by which the vital processes are made possible.

One wonders if God called the angels to inform them of His plans. Did some discussion like this take place?

"Angels, I ask you to look at that little speck of dust over there—it is the earth."

"Yes, Lord, we see it—very small and evidently not of much importance."

"That is the most remarkable of all the billions of worlds that I have scattered across the sky — there is the future home of creatures who will be humans. They will be created 'in the image and likeness of

God.' They must have careful preparation made for them. They must have light and heat of just the right amount. Do you think you could solve this problem?"

No doubt the angels would confess their complete ignorance of the method which God had in mind. Then, it may be, God requested them to look upon another world as He pointed out our sun, and informed them that there was His central heating plant for the earth.

"But, Lord, that is so far away—it must be millions of miles distant."

"Yes, I have measured the distance very carefully—you see I 'set' the sun in the exact position it occupies—92,900,000 miles from the earth. Also I made the sun just the size it is, 866,000 miles in diameter, about 1,300,000 times the size of the little earth, which is just 8,000 miles in diameter. But the earth is the only place where life is possible."

"Do You mean, Lord, that the distant sun will actually heat the earth? It must be very hot to send across that distance enough heat for Thy purpose."

"Yes, the surface temperature is at least 15,000 degrees Fahrenheit, and the internal temperature 50 to 60 million degrees. I shall keep it at that exact point because 10% increase or 10% decrease would result in death to every living thing."

"We have just been thinking, Lord, about the deadly Actinic rays from the sun. Will they not kill Your human creatures?"

"These rays WOULD prove fatal but I have placed a thick blanket of Ozone Gas all around the earth. It begins 15-20 miles above the earth and is thousands of feet in thickness. This will shield My children perfectly."

We can almost hear the angels sing at this juncture some such song as Psalm 145:3, 4:

"Great is the Lord and greatly to be praised;
And His greatness is unsearchable.
One generation shall laud Thy works to another,
And shall declare Thy mighty acts."

And here is one wonder upon another. If the sun were 193,000,000 miles from the earth, the intense cold would kill. If it were 50,000,000 miles distant the awful heat would kill. If the heat were not sufficient or regular —if it were not able to cross the immense distance through the icy regions of stellar space, without losing its heat,—death would be the inevitable result. Here are the indelible "footprints of God."

The sun is a great ball of fire which is consuming itself at the rate of 250,000,000 tons every minute of time but still remains sufficient for God's purposes. Someone has called this a miracle, and it must be just that. Consuming itself but never being consumed—the burning bush of the skies. Some scientists declare that the sun is recreating itself as rapidly as it destroys itself. Only God could bring this about.

The Ozone gas layer is a mighty proof of the Creator's forethought. Could anyone possibly attribute this device to a chance evolutionary process? A wall which prevents death to every living thing, just the right thickness, and exactly the correct defense, gives every evidence of plan.

Science News Letter for March 9, 1935, carried an article on Ozone which is quoted in part:

"The earth's protective layer of Ozone

that cuts down the burning ultra-violet rays from the sun may be tapped by the next stratosphere flight.

"Without the presence of ozone in the stratosphere, life on earth probably would not exist in its present form, because the ultra-violet radiation from the sun affects man and other organisms. Tanning and sunburn are but mild forms of what could occur if ozone were not present in the air.

"Prof. Rudolf Ladenburg of Princeton University, speaking before the joint meeting of the American Physical Society and the Optical Society of America, reviewed recent studies of the earth's ozone layer. He said that instead of being some 31 miles above the region of man the layer appeared to be but 15 miles up. . . .

"There is good evidence that it is not a narrow layer as previously pictured. It probably extends from 60,000 to 100,000 feet, with its maximum concentration coming near 78,000 feet."

Every square inch of the sun's surface emits the energy of 130,000 horsepower. Few power plants can equal the energy of more than 9 square feet of the surface of the sun.

Benson writes about the heat of the sun in a graphic manner. If the sun were frozen over completely to the depth of 64 feet, the sun's heat would melt this solid encasement of ice in one minute.

If an ice-bridge could be formed from the earth to the sun, 2½ miles thick, it would melt in one second and be dissipated into vapor in 8 more seconds. It would require a layer of anthracite coal from 19-24 feet thick over the entire surface of the sun, consumed every hour to provide this amount of heat. And yet at that rate, if the sun were made of solid coal it would last 5,000 years! It is probable that no other sun among the millions of suns has just those rays which animals and plants require.

When we remember that if the earth's orbit around the sun were circular instead of elliptical and if the earth's axis were vertical, day and night would be always and everywhere the same, and the entire year one round of dull and unvarying monotony, we feel there is a mighty Hand behind these adjustments. If our day were, say, only 12 hours instead of 24, or if it were 96, death would be the inevitable consequence of these comparatively slight changes. Only an Omniscient Creator could know all these requirements and be able to operate them.

CHAPTER SIX

WATER AND AIR

The study of water brings before the student a whole series of wonders. Each molecule of water contains two atoms of Hydrogen and one atom of Oxygen. Hydrogen is the most inflammable gas known and Oxygen is necessary for all conflagrations. Yet when God puts these two gases together they make the best fire-extinguisher known.

All fluids when subjected to cold become slightly heavier. This is true of water until it reaches within four degrees of freezing when instead of increasing its specific gravity, it becomes lighter and rises to the surface as ice is formed. It is not hard to see the reason for this. If ice sank to the bottom as soon as formed, presently all lakes and rivers would be solid and the result would be death to all the living inhabitants. So, by altering the otherwise universal law, God causes ice to be not only non-death dealing, but actually a wonderful protection to the fish in their wintry habitat. Chance? Hardly.

Water in great quantity is needed for all life purposes—vegetable, animal, human. The Great Architect must have made very definite calculations and that is exactly what God's Book tells us. We read in Isaiah 40:12:

> "Who hath measured the waters in the hollow of His hand?"

There are 197,000,000 square miles to the surface of the earth. 145,000,000 square miles are covered with water, and but 52,000,000 square miles are dry land. Man would hardly have arranged it thus.

And the ocean depths are exactly the right size in order to contain this great amount of water. If these basins of the seas were evened up to the surface of the earth, the entire globe would be covered between one and two miles deep in water. That there is design here is suggested strongly in several passages of Scripture.

Genesis 1:9, 10 reads:

"And God said, Let the waters under the heaven be gathered together unto one place, and let the dry land appear; and it was so.

And God called the dry land Earth; and the gathering together of the waters He called Seas: and God saw that it was good."

And again in Psalm 33:7,-:

"He gathereth the waters of the sea together as a heap:
He layeth up the deep in storehouses."

This is definite and very interesting. God excavated "storehouses" just the right size, "gathering" the waters together, and "laying" them up in their appointed places. Could anything be more precise than this? And when we think of it, if this important item had been left to chance what prospect would there have been of human life?

How wonderful is our Lord to think of everything for our comfort, and what a blessing is water! Clear, tasteless, cool, refreshing fluid! When the tongue is dry, the lips parched, the throat feverish, what a delight is a glass of pure cold water, as it trickles over the tongue and gurgles down the throat.

This luxurious beverage is brewed for us by our Heavenly Father—brewed in grassy dells where the deer, the antelope, and the child love to play.

He brews it on the mountain top whose granite peak glistens like gold in the sunlight; He brews it in the depths of the seas and in subterranean caverns.

You see it glistening in the dewdrop and singing in the summer rain; it sparkles in the ice-gem when the trees seem loaded down with rare jewels. It gleams in the hoarfrost struck by the rays of the morning sun.

Hidden snugly in the depths of the evening clouds resting on the western horizon, God paints a gorgeous sunset shimmering with all the hues of heaven until our senses reel with the beauty of it.

The water of life brings energy and refreshment to man and beast and lowly plant. It is one of God's great gifts to the world.

Consider the beauty of a rainbow, which is a circular spectrum. The spherical drops of water falling out of the rain-cloud become prisms by which the rays of light are separated into their primary colors.

A ray falls upon the outer surface of the drop, is refracted or broken from the direct line as it passes through, is then reflected from the opposite inner surface back to the convexity nearest the observer, and passing out of the drop, is once more refracted, and falls upon the observer's eye as a single color of the spectrum.

The eye is so arranged as to receive but one of the colors from any one drop, but from other falling drops it gets the remaining colors.

These innumerable raindrops are divided into seven vast army corps. Each corps will include the drops which produce one of the seven primary colors, and the uniform of a corps will be red, green, blue, or some other color according to the order.

All the individuals of this army corps are mustered together in one great line of parade stretching around the sky; the red rays appear as an extended line to the observer. Next to this line of red will stretch the battle line of that army corps which wears the orange uniform. And so on through yellow, green, blue, indigo and violet, until the whole united host is mustered rank on rank in beautiful and orderly dress parade over the black background of a receding cloud. The Master-Artist of the universe has put on a gorgeous display of beauty.

The water, when measured, weighed, and stored, must be distributed across the face of the earth if its mission is to be carried out. Here is one of the vastly difficult engineering problems confronting the Divine Architect. Water weighs 800 times more than air and yet it must be lifted against the force of gravity, held in suspension above the earth, moved to definite locations, and brought down in gentle refreshing showers bringing life to a thirsty ground. It has been estimated that approximately 16,000,000 tons of water fall every second. Obviously this must have been raised from oceans and lakes and rivers to make its fall possible.

That this great amount of heavy liquid could be raised into the atmosphere would seem to be as impossible as that the gravel from the bottom of a lake should rise and swim on the surface. Yet our God devised a plan which works every day with infinite ease, causing water to climb high into the firmament and float easily at rarified altitudes, three, four and even six or more miles high.

The atmosphere is so constituted that it can absorb moisture and retain it in an invisible state; the warmer it is the greater its capacity to do this.

Hidden away in what seems to be a casual statement in Psalm 135:5-7 is an exciting bit of information in which God reveals to us the solution of this great problem of lifting and distributing the water:

> "For I know that the Lord is great,
> And that our Lord is above all gods.
> Whatsoever the Lord pleased,
> That hath He done,
> In heaven and in earth,
> In the seas and in all deeps;
> Who causeth the vapors to ascend
> From the ends of the earth;
> Who maketh lightnings for the rain;
> Who bringeth forth the wind
> Out of His treasuries."

By the action of the sun's rays water is vaporized—a process known as evaporation. In this state water occupies a space 1600 times greater than in its liquid state, and is therefore much lighter than the atmosphere. Consequently it floats readily and ascends into the higher regions—"He causes the vapor to ascend."

In the higher and cooler altitudes this vapor gradually condenses into visible clouds, sometimes thousands of feet in thickness, and tens of thousands of acres in extent, suspending in their dark folds immense quantities of water ever ready to return to earth. It is obvious that man could neither invent nor operate such an ingenious and gigantic plan for hoisting millions of tons of water from the deep places of the earth, ceaselessly, noiselessly, and in addition, provide for its gentle and regular precipitation throughout the earth.

Solomon, apparently, was puzzled by this problem. When we read Ecclesiastes the first chapter and seventh verse, it seems quite possible that he had been worried regarding the vast torrents of water being emptied from the

Jordan River into the Dead Sea, a body of water without any outlet. It may be he had visited the Dead Sea occasionally to investigate the water level, and now on his return he sits down and writes:

> "All the rivers run into the sea; YET THE SEA IS NOT FULL; unto the place whence the rivers come, thither they return again."

This seems to be quite a pertinent observation—torrents of water emptying daily into this closed basin without any change in the level. And then he answers his own question by saying,—"unto the place whence the rivers come, thither they return again." This is a strange statement. He knew that the tributaries of the Jordan rose in the hills and mountains and says they return to their source. When has anyone seen a river running up hill? And yet this seems to be his meaning. God held his pen that day and he wrote more wisely than possibly he knew. It is true that the waters do go back to the hills and mountains. How can this be?

We look for the answer in Psalm 135 and 7th verse, already quoted. First let us consider how these cloud masses unload their precious cargo. "He maketh (deviseth) lightnings (electrical discharges) in order to produce rain." That there must be electricity in some form in the atmosphere before rainfall is possible is known. In the presence of a tiny particle of dust, the electrical current, in conjunction with proper atmospheric conditions, is able to condense the moisture into a small drop which joins with others until the weight causes it to fall. It is rather astonishing to find this hint of God's process in this Psalm.

In Proverbs 8:26 we read of "the highest part of the dust of the world." Infinite wisdom putting into the upper atmosphere the dust particles necessary for raindrops even before the earth was made! But these must have been carried down to earth long since. How is the dust replenished? And modern astronomy suggests the answer. We are told that at least 20,000,000 blazing meteors from other worlds that can be seen with the naked eye enter our atmosphere every 24 hours and are burned into dust, besides the millions that cannot be seen. Infinitely clever, this!

How is the water that is held in the clouds to be conveyed to the places where needed? "He bringeth the winds out of His treasuries." And what does He say to them? "Winds hitch yourselves to these cloud-chariots and carry them across hill and dale." The beautiful system of air-currents or winds constitutes the mighty arm that impels these immense cloud-masses.

A ship loading with merchandise at a foreign dock or a train starting with freight from a railroad station, is not more explicit in its mission than the movement by the winds of these mountains of water. The currents of air take in from sea and lake and river their precious cargoes of vapor, and scud away with them to the waiting isles and to the hearts of continents, obeying the command of their Creator, and dropping their enriching stores over the dry and parched land.

The entire operation is conducted with amazing accuracy and apparent ease. Think of the admirable way by which God has arranged that the rain should, for the most part, drop in soft and gentle showers. If the clouds poured out their prodigious contents at once in great streams and floods, the consequences would be tragically destructive. Occasionally this does happen with great havoc.

Without the provision for gentle showers, vegetation would be destroyed, crops beaten into the ground, trees stripped of leaves and fruits, fields ploughed into deep trenches, and soil washed away. Every passing cloud would be an object of terror.

But how beneficent is the existing arrangement. Instead of ruinous cascades of water, it trickles down in gentle and fertilizing drops, as if the cloud were perforated like a sieve with tiny openings. The drops fall and seldom is a blade of grass hurt, or the most delicate flower bruised.

It is not possible to view all these adjustments without an exclamation of admiration and gratitude as we behold the wisdom and goodness of God.

An old book by Dr. H. W. Morris, now out of print, but still full of interesting suggestions —called "Work-Days of God," provides many of the thoughts recorded in the pages immediately following, with much new material added.

Snow and hail, like the rain, descend from the great laboratory of the firmament. Snow consists of infinitesimal particles of frozen watery vapor — crystallized water. A snowflake is one of God's most beautiful architectural marvels. It is composed of fine, shining spicula diverging from the centre. Falling through the atmosphere they gather others in their train and thus increase in bulk. Their variety is infinite and all equally beautiful, varying in size from one-third to one-thirtieth of an inch in diameter.

In unnumbered billions these downy flakes are showered upon the earth, every one formed perfectly after its proper model; each particle has its precise place and position,—the great majority six-sided stars, every one in figure and symmetry perfectly geometrical. Who but God possesses a wisdom and skill which enables Him thus to manifest the power to create instantly countless designs exhibiting an infinite beauty of formation causing us to bow in adoration and praise?

The loving forethought of God is seen in the snowflakes. Snow provides a warm blanket for the earth wherever winters are severe. Extreme cold would cause to perish every living thing, so God appointed that the rain which falls in summer to refresh and nourish all vegetation should, in winter, descend like soft wool to cover and protect. Settling like a compact layer, it prevents the internal heat of the ground from escaping.

Also, the rain and snow wash down nitrogen in combination, so that nitrites and nitrates give strength and vigor to growing things. It has been estimated that this is worth each year about $14 an acre. The snow piled high on the mountains serves as an inexhaustible reservoir of water which in the form of gradually melting snow, as summer advances, flows down in grateful supplies to the panting plains below.

This feature reveals the importance of mountains and hills. We begin to realize the meaning of Psa. 65:6:

"By His strength He setteth fast the

mountains, being girded with power."

and Ps. 95:4:

"The heights of the hills are His also."

Mountains exert a definite and important effect on climate by affecting the currents of the atmosphere, mitigating the cold, intercepting the clouds, and shielding extensive districts from the unbroken violence of the storms hurtling down from the north. They seem to have been built up by the Great Architect in selected situations and for specific ends. They direct the course of the winds and extract from the clouds their enriching moisture, retaining this enriching moisture until needed elsewhere. Mountain chains are among the number of great agencies arranged by God to equalize the general temperature of the earth.

To these lofty elevations we must ascribe the credit for the magnificent system of rivers. Mountains are the great condensers of the atmosphere, and the sources of springs, brooks and rivers. The number of these rivers on the globe is very great. In the Old and New World there are said to be nearly 700 principal streams, discharging directly into the ocean.

These rivers with their innumerable tributaries constitute a grand system of drainage, with which the beneficent wisdom of the Creator has furrowed the earth. In Europe we find at least four great rivers. The Rhone, 400 miles long, drains about 7,000 square miles; the Rhine, 700 miles in length, carries to the sea the waters from about 15,000 square miles; the Danube pursues its course for 1,800 miles, taking the waters from an expanse of not less than 55,000 square miles; while the 2,100-mile long Volga, winding slowly along its course, gathers the waters of one-half of the great Russian Empire.

Asia has a still more magnificent system. China has two rivers each more than 3,000 miles long, and Siberia two others of equal size. In Siam there are the Iriwaddi and Maykaung, while in western Asia are the Euphrates and Tigris of ancient memory.

British India has large rivers running for thousands of miles, the most celebrated being the Ganges which leaps into sight for the first time from a perpendicular wall of ice in the Himalayas, and pursuing a course of almost

1,900 miles, draws its "sacred" waters from a district of unequalled fertility, embracing an area of not less than 400,000 square miles.

Africa has comparatively few rivers, the Niger stretching its crooked length for 2,000 miles, and the Nile 3,200 miles long, for the last 800 miles receiving not a single tributary.

In America we find rivers of supreme magnitude and grandeur. The St. Lawrence drains 300,000 square miles; the Mississippi, 4,000 miles long, draws its waters from a surface of 1,000,000 square miles. The Amazon is king of them all and near its mouth presents a stream 100 miles wide and 600 feet deep.

In the rivers we have a system of drainage and irrigation of enormous amplitude worthy of Him who scooped out their channels and taught them all their devious ways to the deep. The benefits derived from this network of rivers are obviously incalculable. Besides draining the earth of its surplus waters, without which some of the fairest portions of its surface would soon be submerged, they are the means by which living creatures on the dry land are furnished with their needed drink, and man is given a most valuable food supply in the fish bred in the waters.

They also open great channels of commerce with distant and interior countries; while, in their course to the sea, they provide unlimited power and facilities for manufacture. Rivers have built and have furnished the wealth of the most renowned cities of earth, where the richest monuments of art and industry have been assembled.

Thebes and Memphis owed their splendor to the Nile; Babylon, its birth and greatness to the Euphrates. The Orontes furnished the site of Antioch; the Tiber founded and erected ancient Rome. The Thames has given to England its London, and our own magnificent rivers have built for us some of the richest and busiest cities of the land.

Rivers add greatly to the beauty of our world. God loves them and in a not distant future will give us cause to rejoice in what He will do with them. Isa. 33:21 tells us that "there the glorious Lord will be to us a place of broad rivers and streams." In the supreme climax of eternity, we read in Rev. 22:1 of "a pure river of water, clear as crystal, proceeding out of the throne of God and of the Lamb."

There are ocean rivers which flow as definitely and as regularly as the Danube or the Nile. Their channels are established for thousands of miles as they pursue their course along beds and between banks of other and different water, as fixed as if built of granite rock.

The most remarkable of these is the famous Gulf Stream, so named because it was long supposed to originate in the Gulf of Mexico. Its exact origin is not yet fully known, but Humboldt and others believe that it receives its first impulse near the southern extremity of Africa.

From the Gulf of Mexico this stream flows into the Atlantic between Florida and Cuba, whence it runs northward nearly parallel to the coast of the United States, until it reaches Nova Scotia and Newfoundland, where it makes a great bend, throwing one branch downwards toward the Azores, while the other spreads out and flows north to the British Isles, and thence to the Polar Sea.

The banks and bottom of this magnificent river are of cold water while its main stream is warm. It is 70 miles wide, three thousand feet deep and equal in volume to more than a thousand Mississippis at full flood. In the Gulf of Florida its speed is about 80 miles a day, but by the time it has reached the Azores it has slowed down to 10 miles a day. Its color, as far as the coasts of the Carolinas, is indigo blue; its banks or edges are well defined with the middle of the stream considerably higher than the edges, so that it runs like a serpentine ridge upon the surface of the ocean.

What is still more remarkable, it runs up hill; in part of its course the gradient of its bed is not less than five or six feet to the mile.

Its most notable characteristic is its effect on climate due to its high temperature. As it leaves the Gulf of Mexico, its temperature is 86 degrees. After traversing 10 degrees of latitude it remains at 84 degrees; when it has travelled 3,000 miles north it still preserves in winter, the heat of summer.

Continuing its course it overflows its liquid banks and spreads over thousands of square miles a mantle of warmth. This heat is carried by the west winds over all the west coast of Europe softening and ameliorating its climate.

Thus the British Isles are made habitable, even though in the same latitude as Labrador which is bound in the grip of ice and snow. Life is made possible in Norway and Sweden where otherwise eternal cold would prevail.

One writer, Hopkins, says:

"If a change were to take place in the configuration of the surface of the globe so as to admit the passage of this current directly into the Pacific, across the existing Isthmus of Panama, or along the base of the Rocky Mountains into the North Sea—a change indefinitely small in comparison to those which have heretofore taken place — our mountains which now present to us the ever-varying beauties of successive seasons would become the unvarying abodes of the glacier and regions of the snowstorm; the culture of our soil could no longer be maintained, and civilization itself would retreat before the invasion of such physical barbarism."

In view of these considerations are we not justified in believing that the Gulf Stream is another evidence of our God's design and forethought?

Scarcely less remarkable is the Japanese Current which runs along the Pacific Coast and has a somewhat similar effect there. Then there is the great Polar Stream bearing down in the opposite direction to the Gulf Stream—a sort of compensatory current. This rises in the distant recesses of Baffin's Bay and the Greenland Sea and, studded with icebergs, sweeps along the coast of Labrador, encircling the island of Newfoundland in its chill embrace. As it journeys south it encounters the Gulf Stream running northeastward. As the paths of these two giants cross each other, they seem to struggle for right of way. Their hostile waters refuse to mingle and each continues to retain its color and temperature.

From the force of the shock, the Gulf Stream falters in its course, momentarily, and is deflected towards the south. The Polar current, unable to break through the mass of water in the Gulf Stream, dives under its bed and hastens on to the tropics,—bringing its refreshing coolness to these heat-ridden countries.

It is obvious that by reason of this perpetual circulation of the waters of the deep — the streams from and towards the equator—not only is the rigorous cold of the polar regions relieved, but the exhausting heat of the tropics is modified.

There is another interesting fact. The streams which flow from the Polar Seas towards the south carry along with them vast numbers of excellent fish from the colder latitudes. In this way there is supplied to the people of the warmer regions food which could not be found in the heated waters of the southern areas.

As we view our globe in its outlines of land and water, with its manifold and complicated arrangements, we are able to see a bit of God's mind as He formed and fashioned, measured and weighed, and imposed His Divine will on all the details of this marvellous system. When the waters gathered themselves, it was not at random, but in strict conformity to His plan. When the various currents devised by Him began to circulate, there was no chance but rather Omniscience in action. No wonder God pronounced everything "good."

Morris writes suggestively in this way:

> "In the process of the world's creation, every step taken had respect to something beyond itself, while the whole had reference to man, its coming occupant. In adjusting the various agencies that combine to produce the currents and streams of the ocean, the Creator was deciding the inheritance, and in no small measure also, the character and history of nations yet unborn. How unsearchable are His counsels and His ways past finding out!
>
> As He was describing the shore curves, which were to bound the Gulf of Mexico on one side of the Atlantic, He was gradduating the temperature that was to prevail in Great Britain on the other.
>
> Had the course of the stream issuing from that Gulf been directed to breathe its genial warmth on the coasts of Labrador, instead of the British Isles, how different had been the respective histories of the inhabitants of these two countries —how different, indeed, had been the history of the world.
>
> But for each, the times and bounds were before appointed."

When our earth shall have passed through

its final transformation and been made the fitting abode of holiness, we read that there will be "no more sea." This will necessitate an entirely different arrangement. As now constituted, without water, the stillness of death would rule everywhere. But we know that He who is infinite in wisdom and power can introduce new elements, new combinations, and a new atmosphere, clothing the earth with new beauties such as never bloomed in Eden, which neither "eye hath seen nor ear heard, nor ever entered into the heart of man."

The Atmosphere

We live at the bottom of a vast ocean of air which extends to a height of about 200 miles. Man's exploration of this huge expanse has been confined to extremely narrow limits. He has ascended about nine miles in an airplane, and about thirteen miles in a balloon, while the greatest height ever reached by a sounding balloon is only about 24 miles.

The density of our gaseous envelope is greatest near the earth's surface, and gradually becomes thinner as the altitude increases.

About half its weight is within four miles of the earth, although minute traces of air are believed to exist even at a height of 2,000 miles.

The weight of the atmosphere is a very important item about which there could be no chance. The air-pressure at sea level is nearly fifteen pounds to every square inch of surface—an average of fourteen tons upon every person. About one ton of air rests upon every square foot of surface.

This exact weight is due, obviously, to two factors, the weight of the gases composing the atmosphere, and the height to which the air goes. A slight change in either of these conditions might result in a greatly increased pressure or on the other hand, greatly reduced. The former would crush by its weight and the latter would bring about death, possibly through hemorrhage and also inability to breathe the rarified air as on top of the highest mountains.

Of course in addition to these two factors is the presence of watery vapor, another condition on which life depends. And behind all these must be placed the size and weight of the earth determining the atmospheric mantle.

If the weight and size of the earth were doubled every object would have its weight doubled. The atmosphere would press down with twofold force, respiration would be labored and painful. Water would weigh twice as much and sap could not ascend. Tools and implements would be so heavy that they would be unwieldy, every mechanical operation in field and workshop would require twice as much energy. Every animal would move as though loaded down with another of equal size or weight. Men could barely crawl about with strength exhausted in bearing one's own weight.

Winds would tear down all houses if they had not already fallen by their own weight; rain, hail and floods would exert a tremendously destructive force.

If the earth were only half its size and weight—equally death-dealing would be the result with air too light to sustain life. Sap would ascend too rapidly, men and animals would move about very unsteadily and slowly without sufficient ballast. Life could not go on.

These facts cause us to pay attention to the statement in Job 28:24, 25:

> "For He looketh to the ends of the earth,
> and seeth under the whole heaven;
> To make the weight for the winds; He
> weigheth the waters by measure."

How may we account for this remarkable scientific item written down so long ago unless we believe in a supernatural God and in a supernatural Book?

With the exception of water vapor, the percentage of which may vary between wide limits, the constituents of the air are relatively constant in amount. The average composition of dry air is as follows by volume: Nitrogen, 78 per cent, Oxygen, 21 per cent, Carbon Dioxide, .04 per cent, Argon, .96 per cent, with slight traces of Neon, Helium, Krypton, Xenon, Hydrogen and Ozone. In addition, of course, the air contains dust particles, bacteria, and minute quantities of certain gases caused by manufacturing processes,—compounds of Sulphur with Oxygen and Hydrogen.

The constituents of air are not chemically united. They are merely mixed—a device which shows again the wisdom of the Creator.

Think of the two gases which make up 99 per cent of the air—Nitrogen 78 per cent, and Oxygen 21 per cent. Nitrogen serves to dilute the Oxygen thus retarding burning and oxidation, and is necessary as a plant food. Oxygen is necessary for respiration, to support combustion, and to aid decay of organic matter. The delicate balance of these two gases, the constancy of their proportions in the atmosphere, the admirable way in which they operate for their designed purpose must be because there was thought and planning somewhere.

Of the 92 elements known to man not one is more important than oxygen. Man breathes it every moment of the day and night and so is enabled to carry on his life processes. He uses it to help burn the fuels that cook his foods, warm his home and generate power to operate his machinery. He depends on oxygen to decay waste materials, destroy germs, and purify water. In hospitals, submarines, mines and airplanes it is put to vitally important uses.

Nitrogen is by far the most abundant substance in the air. It is an inert or "lazy" gas not combining readily with other substances. The fact that it is abundant and inert is seen to be very necessary. If the air were composed entirely or largely of oxygen, all burning would take place with extreme vigor, and it would be practically impossible to control a fire, once started. Nitrogen, therefore, dilutes the oxygen to the point where it is just active enough for our needs. How was this proportion arranged? Certainly not chance!

Nitrogen is an important constituent of all plants and animals. But most living things are unable to extract it from the vast atmospheric reservoir about them. They depend on certain tiny plants, belonging to the bacteria class, which have the ability to extract nitrogen directly from the air. In this way, nitrogen is made available for all other living things. And man has now succeeded in tapping the great stores of nitrogen in the air by using powerful electric currents, a process known as fixation of nitrogen.

We have just noticed that nitrogen is made available by small plants and this seems to be a remarkable provision of Omniscience. Plants and animals need this gas in order to build protein, an essential substance present in the tissues and organs of all living things. Corn, wheat, oats, and all other common crops remove great quantities of this element from the soil. This may be replaced of course by artificial fertilizers containing nitrogen in the form of certain chemical compounds with potassium, sodium, and ammonia.

The method by which the nitrogen in the air may be seized upon and appropriated by nature is exceedingly interesting. Certain common leguminous plants, such as beans, peas, clover and alfalfa have attached to their roots certain round structures known as nodules which contain types of bacteria able to convert the inert nitrogen of the air into useful nitrogen compounds. Some of these are absorbed by the plants and the remainder is left in the soil to enrich it. Who would ever imagine that these microscopic organisms could be so useful? Was it accident which placed them in the ground?

The action of lightning is another means of fixing atmospheric nitrogen. During a thunderstorm, small amounts of nitrogen and oxygen are caused to combine, forming compounds that are dissolved by rainwater and carried down to the ground.

The feature which arrests our attention is the ingenious way in which this necessary element is made available for plants, and then for animals and humans. Without it life would not be possible, but while free in vast quantities it must be captured in a very special manner. The plan we have so briefly discussed is admirable in every way.

The gas, Carbon Dioxide, which is the product of combustion in animals and man, must be disposed of, otherwise, as it is breathed out in great quantities and released in other ways, life would become impossible. But here is where the divine plan comes in. The plants are eagerly waiting for every bit we can give them and drink it in eagerly through their wide-open mouths present in countless thousands on their leaves. This will be studied later.

The presence of water vapor in the air is another evidence of design. As we have seen, this vapor is constantly arising from oceans, lakes, rivers, and other bodies of water. When the amount of water vapor in the air becomes excessive, it is changed into rain, snow, hail, fog, dew, or frost, depending on the existing conditions.

The humidity of the air is of great importance to the health of all living things. Without water vapor in the atmosphere over the earth, a condition would exist similar to that known to occur on the moon. The surface of the moon is very hot as the sun shines on it, but immedaitely the sun's rays disappear, heat is succeeded by the most intense cold,—almost 200 degrees below zero. The reason for this is the absence of water vapor which holds in its folds the heat received during the day, gradually releasing it through the hours of the night, but so slowly that man is not caused any suffering. Another blanket may have to be pulled over the bed about 4 a. m., but that is all. If the night were much longer, it is easy to see how death would result. The moisture in the air keeps us warm—God's blanket over His children.

In this connection as we study water vapor our thoughts turn to clouds which God calls in Job 38:9 His "garment" for the earth. As air containing water vapor is carried up into the regions where the temperature is lower than at the earth's surface, a large part of the water condenses, forming great masses of minute droplets. Such a cluster of visible moisture is called a cloud. When the condensation takes place near the earth's surface it is fog.

Clouds are of four general types—each very interesting and beautiful in its own special way.

1. Cirrus clouds are thin, feather-like formations floating at a height of three to ten miles. They are made up of minute crystals.

2. Stratus clouds are flat layers often seen close to the horizon in the early hours of the day. Their average height is about 800 feet.

3. Cumulus clouds are thick mountain-like masses that are often seen on a summer day. They usually float at a height of about

half a mile. Frequently they mass together and produce a thunderstorm.

4. Nimbus clouds are dull gray in color and usually extend unbroken over a wide area. Their height varies between a few hundred feet and a mile. Nimbus clouds are the familiar rain or snow clouds.

The Master-Artist of the universe knows how to decorate His heavens! These beautiful cloud-masses ought to inspire our reverence as we know what they are and Who directs them.

We cannot close this study without a brief mention of winds. Without winds the air would be calm and dead,—noxious and irritating vapors, and objectionable odors would distress and disturb humanity daily. But God's thought went ahead and provided a solution. A wind is a movement of air along the earth's surface. Differences of temperature and air pressure are the two basic factors which produce such movements of air, ranging in intensity from the gentle summer breeze to the dreaded West Indian hurricane.

When air is heated it expands and becomes lighter than that of an adjacent region. Immediately the colder, heavier air flows along the earth's surface to the warmer region, and pushes the lighter air upwards. This air is then carried across through the upper atmosphere where it is cooled. It then descends thus completing its cycle. It is the horizontal movement of air we call wind.

And so difference of pressure and temperature on sea and land causes the delightful and invigorating land and sea breezes. During the day the earth absorbs heat more rapidly than the water. This causes the air over the land to become warmer and lighter than the air over the water. So a cool breeze from the water area flows in toward the land during the afternoon—a sea breeze.

At night the land loses heat more rapidly than the water thus causing the air over the water to become warmer and lighter than the air over the land. Consequently there is a flow of colder, heavier air during the night and early morning hours from the land to the water—the land breeze. What a beneficent arrangement by a loving Creator!

The great differences in temperature and air pressure between the equatorial and polar regions give rise to large-scale movements of air. These movements are modified by the rotation of the earth, thus establishing a system of alternating wind belts and belts of calm over the earth's surface.

Of these various belts the trade winds are perhaps the most interesting and certainly they are very beneficial as a means of transportation. There are regions on either side of the equator in which the air is moving steadily from both sides toward the equator. The rotation of the earth causes a deflection of the winds, so that they flow from the northeast in the northern hemisphere, and from the southeast in the southern hemisphere. Ships navigating these areas can always count on the presence of these trade winds.

CHAPTER SEVEN

PLANT LIFE

It is interesting to note again the definite and logical order of creation as recorded in the first chapter of Genesis. The beautiful and perfect creation of the first verse—"In the beginning God created the heavens and the earth," containing plants and animals, and existing for unknown ages, was destroyed by the tremendous cosmic cataclysm of the second verse—"And the earth became waste and void and darkness was upon the face of the deep." This catastrophe, obviously of stupendous character, suggests the first flood and possibly the beginning of the ice-age. It would appear to be the result of the Devil's hatred of God when he was thrown or "cast" to the ground as we are informed in Ezek. 28:17.

In any case, there was stygian darkness and a world covered with water, torn and disordered by the mighty power of one who wished to destroy God's work. There is no reason to think that God would thus annihilate a beautiful world in which sin had not yet entered.

As light is necessary for all life, it is commanded to shine on the first day of this period of re-creation. It was a dim twilight, but was enough for God's purpose. On the second day, the earth's atmosphere was brought into existence as we have noticed in the previous chapter, evaporation with all its possibilities appears under the command of God, as well as the various other arrangements which are necessary before life can survive.

On the third day the continents of the earth were brought up from the ocean depths as the water surged to the "storehouses" which the Creator had prepared for them (Psalm 33:17). Now it is time for vegetation to appear in all the varied forms which were to cover the ground.

> "And God said, Let the earth put forth grass, herbs yielding seed, and fruit trees bearing fruit after their kind, wherein is the seed thereof, upon the earth: and it was so. And the earth brought forth grass,

herbs yielding seed after their kind, and trees bearing fruit, wherein is the seed thereof, after their kind: and God saw that it was good." (Gen. 1:11, 12.)

The above botanical classification is remarkable for its simplicity and its up-to-dateness, the three great phyla mentioned including all that modern science knows. Science uses more ornate language and mentions four groups, Thallophyta, Bryophyta, Pteridophyta, and Spermatophyta, which include the great number of simple plants, with and without chlorophyll such as algae and fungi, up through the various forms until we come to Gymnosperms and Angiosperms, which are the most highly developed classes of the plant kingdom.

That Moses could have been so skilled in the science of botany as to write down correctly these facts on plant life, without the help of the Creator, is unthinkable.

That these various plants did not come from seeds, through an evolutionary process, long-drawn-out, is seen from Gen. 2:5:

"And no plant of the field was yet in the earth, and no herb of the field had yet sprung up: for the Lord God had not yet caused it to rain upon the earth; and there was not a man to till the ground."

That means, obviously, that God using His divine power created the plants fully formed and placed them in the soil where they proceeded to grow and reproduce themselves precisely as they do today.

The loving thoughtfulness of our God is seen in the great variety of all kinds of vegetation, giving us such a wide assortment of grasses, woods, vegetables and fruits. It is also clearly recognized that He made provision for wide variations within the types but made it impossible for one kind to develop into another kind. All must reproduce "after its kind." This great Law effectively prevents the evolutionary changes which an infidel science rejecting Creation imagines must have taken place through long millions of years.

These acts of God were instantaneous—"He spake and it was done; He commanded and it stood fast." Wonderful Creator—the Lord Jesus Christ!

The strange powers conferred upon these living things, in order to insure their continuance by making possible wide distribution of seeds, and in many cases remarkable provision for the life of the seed, show again the inventive genius—to use human terminology—of our God.

In the blackberry and raspberry, for instance, the Engineer devised an indigestible pit around each seed. These pits permit the seeds to pass through the digestive canal in their original condition. Animals eating the berries merely serve to transport the seeds to places other than where the fruit was found.

Sometimes the rinds or seeds themselves are poisonous both to animals and men, and this serves as a warning. At other times the rind is simply unpalatable and discourages a marauder from penetrating further.

The mechanical devices adopted for the transportation of seed are most striking. The tumbleweed with its feathery structure is able to roll along the ground for long distances. Carried by the wind the fruit breaks off and is deposited far from the parent plant.

Then, aeronautics are commonplace in nature. The Chinese Lantern is the familiar red plant used as an ornament in many modern homes. Its inflated calyx surrounds the fruit, which when it has ripened is carried high into the air.

Winged fruits or seed were the precursors of airplanes. The single-winged product of the ash, or the double-winged fruit of the maple, are so constructed that they will fly long distances in order to provide for germination away from the parent. The ailanthus bears a fruit which has a simple propeller.

The common milkweed and dandelion surprise us with their parachutes. The fruits bearing the seeds are wafted high in air and carried miles away from their birthplace.

Usually flowers use air currents for the transference of their pollen. If you doubt this ask a hay fever sufferer! These pollen grains are very lightweight; in the case of pines, there is an appendage attached—a kind of air-sac.

Many of our common native plants have mechanisms for releasing their seed—the envy of our modern engineers. The violet and columbine open their pods by means of valves, one to each pod from which the seeds spring with great force. The mustard plant splits its pods in a peculiar fashion, from the bottom upward, leaving behind a false partition, used for decorative effect. In some species this is beautifully dyed.

The evening primrose has a capsule which splits along four sutures, and from such a "trap" only a few seeds are allowed to escape at a time, thus insuring economy. The jimson weed or thornapple has a similar device.

The poppy, at the time of maturity, has small windows or pores at the apex of the capsule. As the wind blows the long stem of the plant back and forth, the very light seeds are blown out of the pods a few at a time.

In plants like the jewel weed or touch-me-not, the seeds are forced out by spring-like gadgets. A slight jar causes the fruit to shoot its seeds quite long distances. The witchhazel also ejects its seeds with great force, sending them as far as 20 feet.

The lowly mushroom uses a spring to project its spores through the darkness to some small ray of light. Ferns scatter their spores by means of trigger-like devices on the under side of their fronds. The wild geranium uses a catapult to distribute its seeds. Each of the five seeds has its own private mechanism.

The squirting cucumber of southern Europe is very curious. Its fleshy fruit hangs from a stalk which acts as a stopper at one end. As the fruit matures, the cork-like plug pulls loose and the seeds are shot out with great violence because of the internal pressure accumulated throughout the growing season. In America, the wild balsam apple, a climbing annual, follows a similar plan.

There are certain insect-eating-plants which must have a special device. These usually are provided with a spring-like mechanism. Familiar examples are the Pitcher plant, the Sundew and Venus' Flytrap.

The first mentioned has modified leaves forming a structure which resembles a pitcher and collects rain water. The plant nectar sweetens this water, making it attractive to insects. On the inside of the pitcher which is open at the top, there are stiff hairs pointing downward. The thirsty insect enters the pitcher, takes its drink and prepares to leave but finds the way blocked by the hairs and is drowned. The plant now enjoys its meal leisurely.

The Sundew is provided with tiny hairs on the upper surface of its leaves, the hairs secreting a sticky substance from glands located on their tips. This liquid looks like dew but when the insect alights on it to enjoy the morning dewdrop it sticks fast. The hairs then bend toward the middle of the leaf, which closes and traps the insect. The Sundew has its meal.

The leaves of the Venus' Flytrap have two halves, hinged together. On the surface of the leaves are hair-like structures which act like triggers. When the worm or fly crawls over these tiny bristles an immediate impulse is carried to the leaves, resulting in instant closure of the leaves, their hinges permitting this remarkable response.

The sensitive plants, such as the common mimosa, close their compound leaves in mechanical fashion as the result of excessive heat, shock, or the onset of darkness. The huckleberry shoots its pollen from double-barrelled shotguns.

Some pollen grains are rough or adhesive, causing them to adhere to the body or hairs of insects and animals. The stigmas of most flowers are made sticky in order to catch and hold in place the pollen, allowing it to germinate.

Some common weeds distribute their seeds by supplying them with tiny hooks which cling to the hair or fur of animals. Examples are the cocklebur, the common burdock or "sticker," the bur marigold or beggar's tick, and the trefoil or "stick-tight." Each bears hooked or barbed prongs and is loosely attached to the parent plant at maturity. Contact with some animal easily pulls it out and it is given a "free ride."

Coconuts, palm nuts, Solomon's seal and many other fruits prefer water transportation and are so constructed that they will be safely carried to some distant shore without sinking.

Let us ask again—"Who but God could

devise such an amazing array of unique devices as we have enumerated?"

The wonderful way by which the pollen grains of the cornstalk reach their destination—the kernel of corn on the cob—is worthy of attention. The two obvious features of this common plant are the drooping tassel at the top and the mass of silk-like threads protruding from the end of the cob encased so carefully in layers of green leaves. The pollen grains—the male element—fall downwards and are caught by the threads issuing from the cob. These are made sticky in order to catch the tiny grains. When a pollen grain adheres to the thread its work has just begun. Somehow or other it must get transportation down to the kernel which it is to fertilize in order to make possible the perpetuation of the cornstalk.

How can it travel along this thread—there is no bus service, no train running, but that does not worry the little grain of pollen. It calmly proceeds to bore a hole in the thread and gradually works its way into the cob, turning the thread into a tunnel along which it travels until it reaches the right kernel. If it could speak it might say: "Good morning, mamma, I've arrived. It was quite a trip down and it's good to be at home!"

Think of the ingenuity and power of an insignificant watermelon seed, which, when dried, weighs only one five-thousandth of a pound, the same weight as a honey-bee. Who would ever imagine what this seed can accomplish under suitable conditions?

Place it in the ground, moisten with the dews of heaven, warm it with the rays of the sun, and the little seed becomes a colossus of energy, as well as a marvel of apparent wisdom. Taking off coat and vest with all other encumbering garments, it begins to work. Sending roots down and vine up, it gathers thousands of times its own weight and proceeds to build the melon. Whence comes the plan and the power which gradually produces this luscious fruit of the ground? At first the melon is all covering—almost—green or mottled, then a layer of white, inside of which is a core of pink with hundreds of seeds scattered throughout in order to make certain that other generations of melons will be produced.

How do the roots finds the water, the flavoring extract, the coloring matter? How do they transfer these from the soil through their tissues and up into the vine and out to the growing melon? This process requires a God.

Only a small fraction of the wonders of plant life can be surveyed in this brief chapter. A few additional and interesting features will bring our discussion of vegetation to a close.

Nothing in creation is more astonishing than the unbounded variety of trees, herbs, grasses, that adorn the earth; nothing more clearly exhibits the abounding goodness of the Creator. Nothing that is needed for the life and pleasure of His creatures is wanting. Grasses and herbs in endless diversity, fruit plants and fruit trees, adapted to every climate and soil, provide for man and beast and bird.

Those products of plants which are edible and useful show the unbounded munificence of God. Here is food to nourish, materials to clothe, and medicines to heal. Not only is there abundant provision to meet our actual wants, but an endless variety to gratify our varied tastes and enhance our pleasure.

Our food might have been limited to a few comparatively insipid roots, tubers, and bulbs; God might have made them all of the same taste, or nearly the same. But instead of this we have an interminable variety of fragrance and flavor, wonderfully suited to please the taste, stimulate the appetite, and to yield every desirable nutriment in health and sickness.

Fruit trees and plants might have been confined to one kind of soil, or to one kind of climate; but, instead, they are adapted in one form or another, for all soils, and all climates. All fruits and products might have matured and ripened at the same season, but Divine wisdom has strewn them along in succession through all the months of the summer and there is a fresh and varied supply constantly available.

Psalm 104:14 informs us that:

> "He causeth the grass to grow for the cattle."

This is a simple pronouncement but when we

study it, we discover a fact of great interest and importance.

The general covering of the earth is grass. There are several thousands of varieties of grass listed. This needed food for beasts of the field and forest covers the face of the earth. It grows not only without care or cultivation but in spite of every kind of abuse and violence. Like a living carpet it covers and adorns the face of nature. Self-propagating, self-perpetuating, it supplies the wants of every passing age with undiminished abundance. Trodden upon, fed upon, it still lives. Laid low by the roller, mowed down by the scythe, and crushed with the foot, it only grows with fresher vigor and richer perfume. Buried under ice and snow for months it springs forth again, surviving every abuse, a model of symmetry and strength.

Its color, a soft and pleasant green, shows the thoughtfulness of God. If it had been deep red or brilliant white,—how dazzling and tiring to the eye! A dark blue or black shade would have cast a pall of gloom over the land. Green refreshes the eye and soothes the spirit of man, providing a suitable background for all the varied shades of leaf and flower. Our God is the Great Artist of the universe.

It is impossible to understand the life processes of a plant without knowing something of the structure of roots. So necessary are roots that the Creator has made some remarkable parts for them and given them most important functions. They must absorb water in large quantities—this water containing dissolved minerals which materials are used in the manufacture of starch and other products.

The roots anchor the plant to the ground, often growing deep into the soil, sometimes as far as fifty feet. It has been found that the roots under a two-year-old clump of prairie grass will stretch to about 319 miles. That means that the greater part of the plant is below ground.

The third use of roots is that of storing food, as in the carrot, turnip and beet.

The structure of a root shows beyond any doubt the wisdom of a Creator. It has a skin or epidermal covering in the form of a protective layer, just one cell in thickness. Its cell walls are made of thin, soft membranes of cellulose, which permit the absorption of water and dissolved mineral salts.

In order to secure a greater absorbing surface, roots are equipped with long, slender, delicate projections called root-hairs. Because of their great total surface area and thin walls, they absorb most of the water admitted to the root. Also, they secrete an acid which aids in dissolving minerals.

In the central part or core of the root are found the conducting tubes for carrying the water, some transporting down from the leaf and others from the root upward—a beautiful system, intricate and accurate in its working.

Perhaps the greatest of all marvels is the chemistry of a green leaf. The leaves of a growing plant are arranged in such a way that they have the greatest possible exposure to the sun. There is little overlapping. Blades of grass are thin but grow very long, thus providing an increased area for catching the sun's rays. Plants cultivated indoors tend always to grow in the direction of light. The stems and leaf-stalks often twist about or grow to unusual lengths so that the leaves may receive the necessary sunlight. It is this sunlight which provides the energy for the vitally important process of food manufacture.

This astonishing process is known as photosynthesis. Examine under the microscope the cut edge of a green leaf, and one sees little rooms with the tiny chlorophyll chemists doing their miraculous work. These tiny grains of chlorophyll, under the influence of the sun's energy, are combining the water drawn up from the ground by the roots, and the carbon dioxide drawn in from the air through thousands of wide-open mouths on the under side of the leaf. The water and carbon dioxide are brought together and as the carbon is separated from the oxygen, the latter is released back into the atmosphere, while the carbon is used to make sugar, which is then changed into starch, so necessary for the life of animals and humans.

This process is not understood, so great is its intricacy, but without the strange power of the plant to use the sun's rays and the other materials, no life would be possible.

Not only do the plants return to us oxygen which is needed, but they give out much water into the atmosphere, thus in another way making life possible. Only a small part of the water absorbed by the roots is used by the plant in making the complex food substances, and the excess in the form of vapor is passed out through the leaf. It has been estimated that a tree of average size, on a warm day in summer, throws off nearly 1,000 pounds of water, and that the grass on a vacant city lot puts into the air about a ton of water in the same length of time.

Is it possible to know these things and believe there is no God? "The fool hath said in his heart, there is no God."

CHAPTER EIGHT

ANIMAL LIFE

We have arrived at a fascinating stage of our study, an examination of the living tenants of our globe, infinite in variety, structure, and powers. Here we shall behold scenes of wonder and enchantment. Here we shall see animated and sentient beings, exercising their amazing gifts, disporting themselves in their native elements, proclaiming the praises of Him who created them and by His providence cares and provides for them all.

Let us read God's account of their creation. It is found in Genesis 1:20-25:

> "And God said, let the waters swarm with swarms of living creatures, and let birds fly above the earth in the open firmament of heaven.
>
> And God created the great sea-monsters, and every living creature that moveth, wherewith the waters swarmed, after their kind, and every winged bird after its

kind: and God saw that it was good.

And God blessed them, saying, Be fruitful and multiply, and fill the waters in the seas, and let birds multiply on the earth.

And there was evening and morning, a fifth day.

And God said, Let the earth bring forth living creatures after their kind, cattle, and creeping things, and beasts of the earth after their kind: and it was so.

And God made the beasts of the earth after their kind, and the cattle after their kind, and everything that creepeth upon the ground after its kind: and God saw that it was good."

Here we have the creation of all living things that inhabit the water and that fly through the air, whales, fishes, birds and insects on the fifth day; on the sixth day, cattle, beasts, and creeping things, including herbivorous creatures, the various species of tame and domestic animals, such as sheep and oxen. The carnivorous animals are included under the name, beasts, lions, bears, etc. The creeping things embrace the reptile family, serpents, frogs, etc.

It will be noticed that God made each living creature, "after its kind," implying not only their variety of forms, instincts, and habits, but that each must produce its own kind, and its own kind only, through all successive generations. By this law of the Creator, any evolutionary transmutation of species is seen to be impossible.

It would require many volumes to study all the varied forms of animal life placed in our world, so we select only a few from each class for examination. In each of them we shall discern without difficulty the wisdom of the Creator.

The WHALE family includes not only the animals commonly designated by that name, but also the grampus, porpoise, dolphin, etc. They are remarkable creatures. Like fish they live in the water, but all their internal parts resemble those of land animals. They have lungs, liver, spleen, bladder, and a heart with partitions, pumping red blood throughout their bodies; they breathe air, are viviparous, and suckle their young. They seem to be a connecting link between beasts and fishes, and yet related to neither genetically.

They are the most gigantic animals made by

God. The elephant and rhinoceros are pigmies in comparison. The cachalot or sperm whale often attains the length of sixty or seventy feet, while the common whale has been found more than 100 feet long, and weighing more than 250 tons.

The spinal column is like the trunk of a good sized tree, the individual vertebrae being massive blocks bound together by the toughest ligaments and cartilages. The main artery is a pipe large enough to hold easily a full grown man.

The heart is a great engine of stupendous capacity and power throwing out gallons of blood at every pulsation. The mouth is large enough to engulf a boat with all its crew, its tongue like a vast feather bed where a half dozen men could lie. Its flattened tail is a massive plate of a hundred square feet of marvellous strength, able with one blow to dash to pieces the stoutest boat.

When alarmed or wounded it is able to assume an erect position plunging downward to a depth of 4,000 to 5,000 feet where there is a pressure of about 200,000 tons. Its covering of oily material, called blubber, is from two to three feet thick, preserving the temperature of this warm-blooded animal exposed to the intense cold of the Polar seas, and enabling it to float and even sleep on the surface. Of course this covering is most necessary to protect it against the enormous pressure it sustains at great depths.

There are thousands of different species of fish, from the enormous white shark weighing 10,000 pounds, down to the diminutive minnow. They are of many shapes and structure, many of them exquisitively beautiful in form and color—some of silver hue, some golden, others displaying all the colors of the rainbow.

The Divine Architect gave them a streamlined shape, just suited to swift and easy locomotion through the water. Their symmetry and form, balanced by fins accurately adjusted to weight and habits, and buoyed up by an air-bladder, by the distension or compression of which they can rise or sink at will, propelled by a tail of powerful muscles, present us with an example of God's omniscience.

The covering of fishes is altogether remarkable. Land animals have hair, feathers, bristles, wool, etc., but none of these would be suitable for creatures living in the water. Accordingly the Creator gave to them a coat of mail, clothing them in a complete suit of horny scales, each of which is a wonder in itself. These scales are sometimes joined at the edges, exquisite specimens of mosaic work; more commonly they are arranged like tiles on a house, and covered with a slimy substance, giving them a perfectly smooth surface, making movement easy and keeping them dry!

Their respiration is made possible by means of gills which are long, pointed plates covered with innumerable blood vessels. From the air mixed with the water the haemoglobin of their red blood cells continually extracts oxygen, so that they breathe in water as easily as we do in air.

Their organs of sight show how wise was their Creator. The eyes are placed so as to give them the widest range of vision; they are so constituted that contact with water is no more troublesome to them than air is to us.

To see clearly in the water a convex cornea is needed and that is exactly what they have. They have no lids, but eels burying their heads in sand and mud are furnished with an extra transparent covering to protect the delicate structure.

One of the most curious kind of eyes, revealing the strange forethought of God, is found in a little viviparous fish of the rivers of eastern Asia, the analeps. The ball of each eye is divided horizontally into two hemispheres, a pupil for each half. The upper vision is for long sight and the lower for near sight. With the upper eye it can discern its enemies at a distance, and with the other, find its food near at hand.

Still more wonderful, perhaps, is the eye of a codfish examined under a microscope. Its crystalline lens, never quite half an inch in diameter, is made up of more than 5,000,000 fibres united by more than 60,000,000 teeth!

There is a fish which has long arms, on the under side of which are hundreds of feet, and on the ends of which are eyes. There is one eye also on the end of each arm. This starfish does not swim as other fish do—it walks along the bottom over stones and shells. The common species has five arms using whichever eye happens to be pointing in the desired direction to lead the rest of the body.

The female gaff-topsail fish — Felichthys felis—living in the ocean along the Atlantic Ocean coast of America, lays her eggs, and Daddy catfish comes along and takes them into his capacious mouth. There in that safe refuge they are hatched and the little fish—55 of them—are carried until they are about 3 inches long. Ultimately they grow until they are about two feet in length. The mystery is in the way father manages to live during the 65 days of his parental responsibility.

Two kinds of fish—photoblepharon and anomalops—carry lanterns which are made of luminous plants in the form of a tiny species of bacteria. Just below the eyes of the fish are receptacles especially designed for carrying the lanterns and there is a mechanism for turning the light on and off. Could this be evolution?

The world's champion polygamist is the

tiny fish, 2½ inches long, known as the brook stickleback, getting its name from a series of sharp spines on its back. He builds an enticing nest of algae and plant stems, makes it round, and then smears with a cement secreted from his kidneys. He now has a lovely egg incubator but no eggs. Then he swims away in search of a wife. The first one he selects is driven forcibly to the nest which has a door on each side, and Mrs. Stickleback is not permitted to leave until she has laid her eggs. Then daddy spreads over them a substance called milt.

He repeats this performance several times until his nest is filled to his satisfaction, then stays close by until the babies are born. Where did this instinct arise?

Who will ever understand the mystery of the Chinook salmon? Just before Mother Salmon dies she lays her eggs in shallow water of a fresh-water river which will empty into the Pacific Ocean. The eggs hatch and as fingerlings, the young swim down the stream and disappear in the ocean. For four years they live a free and easy life in the ocean, usually reaching a weight of 20 pounds or even more. Then, driven by a mysterious urge, they begin their thousand-mile journey to the place of their birth. They are going back home —to the place of birth to spawn and die. Nothing can stop them. They eat nothing during the entire trip, fighting their way through rapids and over waterfalls, until they are thin and emaciated, but unconquered. Having arrived at the quiet waters of their early existence they lay their eggs—for the only time during their life—and die.

On birds God fairly lavished His skill and artistry. In many respects birds are the most interesting class of animated nature. In their number and variety we witness another astonishing display of Divine invention and creative power. Species exist by the thousand, all forms and sizes, from the great condor of the Andes to the diminutive humming bird flitting like a ray of colored lightning from flower to flower. Our senses are ravished with the grace and elegance of their forms, the ease and swiftness of their motions, as well as by the beauty and gorgeousness of their plumage, making them the fairest marvels of God's

FOOTPRINTS OF GOD 175

world.

Here design and adaptation are seen everywhere. We stand amazed at their beautifully streamlined shape, their lightness, their covering, their intricate bodily structure most admirably adapted to their manner of life, their muscular power, the music of their song, their nest-building instinct, their ability to travel thousands of miles without chart or compass or guide—everything points Godward.

Let us glance briefly at some of these details. Man has just learned the value and importance of streamlining. It was commonplace with the Creator. As lightness was an essential qualification in order to overcome the force of gravity and enable a heavier-than-air creature to rise easily into the firmament of heaven, we would expect to find in birds some astonishing features. We are not disappointed.

To insure lightness their bones and entire structure are filled with air, as a sponge with water. One author writing on this point says:

> "In birds distinguished for their power of flight, such as the Solangoose, Albatross, and Pelican, the air not only fills their

bones, but surrounds the viscera, insinuates itself between the muscles, and buoys up the entire skin; so that the whole body is inflated like a balloon."

And there is more. The air thus enclosed in the bird's body is heated by its natural temperature some ten or twelve degrees above that in the body of a man, this fact rendering the bird still more buoyant.

This light body cleaves the air with its sharp beak, its smooth coat of overlapping feathers terminating in an expansive tail or rudder, possessing a pair of vigorous wings, so that they are able to move in any desired direction and at varied speeds. They can glide motionless through the air, borne on the wings of wind currents, or they can skim the surface of the waters; they can ascend above the clouds, alight upon the earth and play with the furious gale, defying it to throw them off keel.

Birds able to fly with remarkable ease, and so light they float upon the water like cork, can at the same time dive and glide under water. Here is surely a most striking instance of mechanical design. These birds that have been appointed to seek their food under or in the waters, are furnished with a special set of muscles by which they can contract their body, expelling the air, and making it possible to sink and chase their prey along the bottoms of rivers and pools. This is nothing less than divine contrivance.

The covering given to birds—its lightness, smoothness, warmth and beauty—is worthy of all admiration. The entire feathery covering of a large owl weighs only an ounce and a half. It is a warm protection and especially those birds which spend much of their time on the water are able to make their feathers waterproof by secreting an oil on each feather.

The simplest feather is a marvel of ingenuity. Each one has been measured and weighed, shaped and colored with reference to its particular situation and function. The quill diminishes to a fine point with geometrical precision; it is strengthened by two rolls of tissue and carries barbs and barbules. If these barbules are separated they cling to each other and when the pressure is released they spring back and come together with great accuracy.

The reason is that they are locked together by thousands of the most amazing locks — as many as 1,000,000 found on a large feather. Man cannot construct a feather like this and yet we are asked to believe by an infidel and credulous "science" that our reptilian ancestors were able to accomplish this miracle by changing their scales in some unheard-of way!

Not only is there great diversity in form and stature, but in instincts and habits. Some are of great size and power, able to carry off, while on the wing, a lamb, a kid, or even a small deer; others are extremely small and delicate, scarcely larger than a beetle or a bumblebee. Some dwell on the sea, others on land. Some live on flesh, some on seeds and grasses. Some roost through the night and are abroad in the day; some have the reverse habit. Some make their homes on the loftiest mountain crags, others in the lowest fens and marshes; some in the depths of the forest, and some on the barren, sandy desert. Some like to soar among the clouds, others prefer to dive to the bottom of pools. Some are wild and untamable, others are domesticated and content to dwell about the habitation of man.

This great diversity among the fowls of the air is no more interesting than the fact that every kind of preference can be satisfied because of the varied powers that are conferred on each kind of winged creature. The entire structure and each organ of birds display marked adaptation to their different modes of life.

In every instance, the beak or bill is modified and constructed according as its owner is a swimmer, a wader, a courser, a scratcher, a climber, a percher, or a ravener.

The sparrow subsists principally on seeds and grain, and is given a bill so sharp and a point so well tempered that it can easily pick every kind of seed from tiny places; also it is able to hull them and obtain the precious kernel.

The carnivorous hawk and other similar birds are armed with a hooked beak with which they can separate the flesh from the bones of animals as cleanly as a dissector's knife.

The goose and duck, designed to feed partly on grass and on such substances as may be found in the mud at the bottom of pools, are furnished with a spoon bill, the most suitable that can be imagined for the purpose.

The parrot, a climbing bird, is provided with a beak that carves into a hook, making it easy to climb from twig to twig, and from branch to branch.

The gannet which feeds upon fish has the sides of its bill irregularly jagged in order to hold more securely its slippery victims. The crane lives and seeks its food among the waters. At first thought this would seem to be very difficult for a bird that is without webbed feet and is incapable of swimming. But, to make up for this deficiency, it is given long legs for wading, and a long neck and bill for groping after its food.

The woodpecker, living chiefly on insects lodged in the bodies of decayed trees, is given a bill straight and hard and sharp, to dig and bore after them; and also a tongue which it can thrust out three inches, tipped with a stiff, pointed, bony thorn, barbed like an arrow. Having discovered the abode of the insects, the tongue is given a lightning-like thrust, and the insects are transfixed on the barbed point, and drawn into the mouth of the woodpecker.

Look at the foot of birds. Water fowl have a web foot, the most effective propeller for them in water. Land birds have received what is for them a more suitable foot,—a divided one. The vulture, eagle, hawk, birds that prey on rabbits, mice, etc., are armed with crooked, sharp and powerful claws, with which they can seize and hold in sure grasp whatever they touch. The heron and cormorant have the middle claw toothed and notched like a saw, because, being great fishers, the notches assist in holding the slippery prey.

Of all animals, birds are best equipped for uttering vocal sounds. Their windpipe is large and strong; the larynx, unlike that of man, is double, one being at the top of the trachea and the other at the bottom. The sound produced in the lower larynx is modulated in passing through the upper so that by means of the two they are able to produce nearly all possible variations of sound.

The air supply comes not only from the lungs but from the air-sacs distributed over the entire body. This accounts for their ability to continue for so long their song without stop or interruption. In different species we find these organs of voice modified so as to utter different notes. The cawing of the crow, the croaking of the raven, the cooing of the dove, the carolling of the lark, the warbling of the nightingale, are all the results of their varied organization, modified according to the plan and will of the Infinite Intelligence who created them all.

These little artificers excel in nest-building. Each species seems to be able to select the very locality best suited to its habits and temperament. Hence the situations of nests are as varied as the natures of the builders. Some choose the tufted grass, some the clay bank, some the eaves of houses, some the surface of the sand, some the clefts of the rocks, some the dark and hidden caves. The great majority prefer the bushes and trees.

The main object aimed at seems to be to secure and preserve a sufficient degree of heat for the eggs during the process of incubation. Hence both the character of the materials used,

FOOTPRINTS OF GOD

and the care with which they are put together, vary with the size of the bird, the climate, and the season of the year.

Large birds like the eagle and the osprey, whose great bodies possess in themselves adequate heat without much artificial aid, build carelessly, and with a few rough materials; while the little goldfinch forms the cradle of its young with fine mosses and lichens, made compact as felt, and then lined with thistle-down—beautifully constructed.

The thrush which breeds very early plasters its nest with loam, in order to exclude the cold; the wren waits until mid-summer until nature supplies the necessary heat which her tiny form cannot provide.

The saucy woodpecker displays great ingenuity. After careful examination he selects his tree, cuts out a hole in the solid wood as round as if measured with a pair of compasses. The direction is downward for about six inches on a slanting angle, and then directly down for ten inches more. While shaping this capacious and smooth room, the chips are carried out and scattered at some distance to divert suspicion.

All birds propagate their species by eggs. The number of eggs laid by each particular species has been limited by creative wisdom. Birds of prey lay few and breed slowly; those preyed upon breed rapidly and in great profusion, so that the balance of nature is preserved.

When the nest is finished and the appointed number of eggs laid, the bird is led by some infallible power to sit on them for a definite length of time. Nothing can exceed the patience, self-denial, and endurance of the mother bird while hatching. When she must leave to get food for herself she returns promptly lest her precious charge should become chilled. With tender caution every egg is covered with her body, and frequently moved and turned that all may partake equally of the vital warmth. This is a revelation of the thoughtfulness of the Sovereign Lord of the universe in giving such marvellous instincts to His humble creatures.

The fecundity of birds is a remarkable feature of their powers. We read that "God blessed them, and said, Be fruitful and multiply." As a result of this command, birds are found everywhere in great numbers,—countless millions of them. The great naturalist, Audobon, once estimated that a flock of pigeons which passed over him must have contained more than a thousand millions. That number would require eight million bushels of grain or seed daily.

Their powers of migration excite our wonder. A very large proportion of the different species of birds undertake regularly at certain seasons of the year, long and distant journeys from one clime to another. The general intention of these migrations seems to be to secure a supply of food, and often, a suitable temperature for rearing their young. Some species arrive and depart on the exact day each year. Some choose to travel alone, or in single pairs; some assemble in vast flocks, under appointed leaders. Some travel by day, some by night, while others press on their way without interruption both day and night. What guideposts do they have? What astonishing instinct compels this strange moving each year? Where does it originate? The only satisfactory answer is GOD!

Many books have been written on the curious devices adopted by the various forms of life. Mention is made here of but a very few.

For instance, the female of the king penguin that lives on the island of South Georgia, incubates her egg on the top of her foot. She lays but one egg which is carefully placed on the upper surface of her right webbed foot. The Divine Architect provided her with a special piece of skin flap growing above the foot, and this is pulled down over the egg holding it firmly in place, helping to keep it warm until the baby is hatched.

The tiny humming bird is the strongest of all fliers in proportion to its size. In fact, if it desires to move it must fly because its feet are used only for perching and are so constructed that one cannot be placed ahead of the other as in walking. But this bird can fly in any direction, forward, sidewise, up, down, and even backward. It can poise motionless in the air, a feat which may be noticed by every observer as it thrusts beak and tongue into the flower extracting the delicious nectar.

A visit to the insect world reveals a veritable fairyland. These little creatures—products of the Creator's skill—have been given the most astonishing instincts and mechanical equipment in the whole range of life-forms. They perform impossible feats of magic from the moment of birth. There is no possibility of learning these tricks—they have no teachers and no schools. They spring into action without a moment's delay, doing easily and accurately the same marvellous wonders their ancestors have performed down through the ages. There is no other explanation than creation.

The actions of these life-forms are due to their inherited instincts. Instinct is something which leads an animal to perform certain acts necessary to preserve its life and to propagate its species. In order that instincts may be of real service they must be perfect. They are not and, in the nature of things, cannot be taught or learned. They must be fully developed from the first moment of entrance upon life's activities.

This means that these powers cannot possibly be the result of an evolutionary process.

If there ever was a time when the animals were unable to exercise these mysterious powers they would have died inevitably, and the species would have vanished. The argument from instinct is a rock upon which the theory of evolution is hopelessly shattered.

Although written many years ago, Paley's "Natural Theology" is today one of the most profound and logical discussions of this important theme—the existence of God. In the following pages many of the observations must be credited to this able author and the reader is urged to read the entire book if it can be secured—long out of print.

No attempt is being made, of course, to produce a system of natural history, and only a few of these wonders of instinct will be mentioned. In nature they are innumerable and will richly repay careful study.

Egg-laying and incubating has been mentioned. Let us examine this interesting phenomenon. What causes the mother bird to prepare a nest before she lays her eggs? No one will claim reasoning powers for her. The feeling of fullness which may be discernible to her in a particular portion of her body because of the presence of the egg could not possibly inform her that she was about to produce something which, when produced, was to be preserved and protected. In every other instance, what issued from the body was cast out and rejected.

Then too, when the egg is laid, how could birds know that these eggs contain their young? There is nothing either in the aspect or internal composition of the egg which could lead her to the idea of a living perfect bird coming from the egg.

If we could imagine that the bird's curiosity impelled her to break the shell and examine the contents, what information could she derive from the white of the egg? Could she see in that portion the outline of feathers and other materials? If, after sitting on the eggs for a few days, she again breaks the shell, what significance would there be to her in the red streaks which would be visible? Would she imagine that these were ultimately to become bones and limbs?

Who, seeing the minute pulsating point

which appears after only two days of incubation, could possibly anticipate that it was soon to become a heart, and the centre of a complete circulation?

For the sake of the argument, let us admit that the sparrow might in some mysterious manner have arrived at the conclusion that within that egg lies concealed the making of a future bird. From what chemical expert is she to learn that warmth is necessary to bring it to maturity? How can she know that the degree of heat imparted by the temperature of her own body is the exact degree required?

To suppose, therefore, that the female bird acts in response to a reasoning capacity, is to say that she arrives at conclusions wholly unjustified by any apparent facts in the case. If the sparrow, sitting upon her eggs, expects young sparrows to emerge, she indulges in what would seem to be a wild and extravagant expectation, in direct opposition to all appearances and probabilities.

To do this, she must have penetrated into the mysteries of biology further than any of our faculties will carry us. And, it is apparent, that this sagacity—if it be such—exists side by side with great stupidity.

Another old writer, Addison, writing on this point, says:

> "A chemical operation could not be followed with greater art or diligence than is seen in hatching a chicken; yet the process is carried out without the least glimmering of thought or common sense. The hen will mistake a piece of chalk for an egg; is insensible of the increase or diminution of their number; does not distinguish between her own and those of another species; is frightened when her supposititious breed of ducklings take to the water."

Why do moths and butterflies deposit their eggs on certain kinds of leaves, cabbage for example? Although they themselves cannot taste nor use the cabbage-leaf, yet this is the appropriate food for the young larvae as soon as they emerge from the eggs. How do the parents arrive at this knowledge? Certainly not through education, and just as certainly not through chance. This instinct—a gift from the Creator—leads them instinctively to do this very necessary act in order that their young may survive.

Among many kinds of caterpillar forms there are cabbage-caterpillars and willow-caterpillars. Never will there be found cabbage-caterpillar eggs placed on willows, nor the reverse. This needs explanation if God be eliminated.

The butterfly had no teacher in her caterpillar state. She never knew her parent. Any knowledge acquired by experience could not be transmitted from one generation to another. There is no opportunity either for instruction or imitation. The parent race has vanished before the new brood is hatched. If it is original reasoning in the butterfly, then what a profound mentality we attribute to this winged creature! She must remember her caterpillar state, its tastes and habits; of which memory, however, she shows no signs.

She must conclude from analogy that the little round body—the egg—which drops from her abdomen, will at a future period produce a living thing, not like herself, but like the caterpillar which she remembers herself once to have been. Under the influence of these deep reflections she seeks to provide for an order of things which she concludes will, at some time or other, take place. This must be true, also, not only of a few butterflies but of all.

These factors, it must be acknowledged, are far too intricate for the imagination to envision. In these we must see the intervention of the Creator.

There is yet another inexplicable puzzle to be solved. How shall we account for that which is the source and foundation of all these phenomena, the apparent parental affection, which can only be explained by instinct?

No one would contend that the attitude of these animals towards their offspring comes from a sense of duty, or of decency, a care for reputation, a compliance with what is considered good public manners or laws, or with certain rules of life built upon a long experience of their utility.

Why should the bird pay so much attention to the egg? As we have noted, everything else proceeding from the body is cast away and rejected. Is it the egg which the hen-bird loves? Or is it because she fondly anticipates the joy of a future progeny that she clings so faithfully to her nest, carefully covering and protecting the things which fill her abode? Why should a brooding hen look for pleasure from her chickens—yet unborn?

The mother cuckoo never sees her babies because she deposits her eggs in a strange nest refusing to perform the labor of building for herself. Yet, in her way, she is as careful in making provision for them as any other bird. She does not leave her egg in any convenient hole. She finds a satisfactory nest already constructed, then lays her eggs, and forgets all about the operation.

It will hardly be argued that the butterfly has such accurate knowledge of "the shape of things to come," and such deep parental affection that she diligently searches out just the right kind of leaf upon which the grub which she will never see, and of which she knows nothing, is to feed and preserve its life.

Nor can it be that she has a genuine but

abstract anxiety for the general preservation of the species, a sort of patriotism, a real solicitude lest the butterfly race should disappear from the face of the earth.

Maternal instinct is as necessary for the preservation of life as the sensation of hunger. The only rational explanation is that this is an original endowment for a special purpose, by the Creator.

Another question arises. Why should this parental affection disappear when the young animal has grown up? Association of parent and child operating in its usual way ought to produce the contrary effect. But this is not the case. After a certain time, birds and beasts banish their offspring; they disown their acquaintance and seem to have no knowledge of the objects recently absorbing their solicitous care, and occupying the industry and labor of their bodies.

This change in attitude, it must be noted, takes place at differing distances of time from birth; but the time always corresponds with the ability of the young animal to support itself. It never anticipates it.

In the sparrow tribe, when the young brood can fly and shift for themselves, the parents forsake them forever; and although they continue to live together, they pay no more attention to them than they do to other birds in the same flock. The parental care exists only when it is needed. If this be not the result of intelligent reasoning—and it cannot be due to that—then only instinct remains as the solution. And instinct belongs to God.

Those who admit the wonders of egg-laying and protection and yet deny that creative forethought has anything to do with the operations, offer a naive explanation. We are gravely informed that the bird engaged in incubating the eggs derives real pleasure from the pressure of the smooth convex surface of the shells against her abdomen. At this particular time the body of the bird is abnormally heated and the cool and smooth egg-shell gives her an agreeable sensation.

Thus, so goes the story, present gratification is the only motive with the hen for sitting upon her nest; the hatching of the chickens is to her an accidental circumstance.

Let it be allowed, if necessary, that the hen is induced to brood upon her eggs because of the relief she experiences from the pressure of round smooth surfaces against her overheated skin. Will some one inform us how it happens that this extraordinary heat is felt at the exact time when it is needed to hatch the eggs? And also we would like to know why this time tallies so exactly with the internal constitution of the egg, and with the urgent need to bring it to maturity?

Design is everywhere apparent in this study, and back of the design, let it again be said, must be the Designer.

Let us quote a paragraph or two from Paley. He writes:

> "Neither ought it to be forgotten how much the instinct costs the animal which feels it; how much a bird, for example, gives up by sitting upon her nest; how repugnant it is to her organization, her habits, and her pleasures. An animal formed for liberty submits to confinement in the very season when everything invites her abroad; what is more, an animal delighting in motion, made for motion, all whose motions are so easy and so free,

> hardly a moment at other times at rest, is for many hours of many days together, fixed to her nest, as close as if her limbs were tied down by pins and wires. For my part I never see a bird in that situation, but I recognize an invisible hand, detaining the contented prisoner from her fields and groves, for the purpose, as the event proves, the most worthy of the sacrifice, the most important, the most beneficial.
>
> But the loss of liberty is not the whole of what the bird suffers. Harvey tells us that he has often found the female wasted to skin and bone by sitting upon her eggs. . . ."

Surely these are important and suggestive considerations. The conclusions to which these irrefutable facts lead bring us face to face with a Supreme Intelligence.

Innumerable examples of mysterious and almost miraculous powers abound in the animal world. Everywhere we turn we are face to face with the supernatural. We are able to study only a very few of these exceedingly interesting life-forms.

The story of the marvels of the honeybee has furnished material for many books on the subject. This tiny parcel of life, weighing only about one five-thousandth of a pound, one-half inch long, one-quarter inch high, is the possessor of an amazing variety of organs and powers.

Inside that body is a chemical factory whose intricate operations stagger us with their perfection. The bee is equipped with an elaborate tool kit with which it performs unheard-of feats; as with other insects it has three pairs of legs, and from front to rear is divided into three sections. There is the head, carrying the antennae, the mouth, the eyes and the brain; the mid-section or thorax provides attachment for legs and wings; while the abdomen holds the reproductive organs, the heart, the digestive organs, and the sting.

Each of the parts mentioned has a very special construction adapted to its particular use. The antennae extending out in front are smellers rather than feelers. They are the noses of the bees, a most necessary part since bees are guided in their everyday work largely by smell. It is thought that each individual member of the colony has its own distinct odor, so that recognition of one another comes in this way. On the ends of the antennae are thousands of sense plates. The queen which leaves the hive so infrequently and does not need acute smelling powers has only about 2,000 of these sense plates on her two antennae. A worker bee, hunting for new sources of nectar in the flowers and depending on this power, has as many as 6,000. The drone needing the sense of smell to find his mate may have 30,000.

The eyes of the bee are five in number, two large ones on the sides of the head, and three smaller ones between the two main organs of sight. The two large eyes are compound, composed of thousands of tiny six-sided lenses, used probably in perceiving distant objects while the simple eyes are used for near sight. The bee's eye is a fixed-focus camera, and without eyelids, so that the bee must sleep with its eyes always open. The bee is color-blind to red but is able to see ultra-violet rays which are invisible to us.

Bees seem to be comparatively deaf to sounds but are very sensitive to physical vibrations. The tongue of the bee has been described as fashioned like some fantastic Chinese weapon, a beautiful and delicate tube through which the nectar from the flowers is sucked into the mouth and stomach. The taste sense of this insect seems to be well developed.

The wings and legs found on the mid-section are specially constructed. The wings are wonderfully efficient enabling the bee to navigate the air at 15 miles an hour, carrying loads many times heavier than itself so astonishing is their strength. Each bee has four wings, two large front ones, and two smaller ones in the rear. When the bee is at rest or entering the hive, they overlap, thus taking up less room and just fitting the six-sided cell into which it must partially enter. In flight a strange change takes place so that they function as a single pair, the rear ones becoming attached by small hooks to a ridge or cleat running along the rear edge of the front wings. Could evolution accomplish this strange device?

In flight the bee vibrates its wings 11,140 times a minute—190 times a second—and is complete master of the air. They can fly forward, back, up and down, side to side, and poise motionless like a helicopter, only much more perfectly.

The equipment given to the legs of the honeybee is one of the most complex tool-kits in all the realm of natural history. On the front legs are antennae cleaners, a self-threading needle arrangement, one on each side, with a little horny piece which can be lifted to permit the antenna of the opposite side to enter. Immediately on the outside of this we see a series of stakes, or teeth of a comb,—hairs made for cleaning the antenna as it is slipped back and forth. This action removes dust and dirt and keeps the smelling apparatus in working condition.

On the middle pair of legs are sharp spurs, like an elephant's tusk, or a crowbar, used to pack pollen in the pollen baskets on the hind legs, and to pry it out when home is reached.

On the outside of the flattened hind legs are depressions known as "pollen baskets," permitting the insects to bring home large masses of pollen. Inside the hind legs are side-combs which are constantly sweeping over the bee's hairy body gathering the pollen dust and then emptying it into the "basket" by running the teeth of the comb over stiff hairs surrounding the pollen basket. The dust drops in, is packed down with the spur. Also on the hind legs there are the so-called wax-shears between two of the joints used for clipping the wax as it comes from the body of the bee, secreted by mysterious glands inside and deposited on eight waxplates — four on each side of a central "keel" which runs along the bottom of the rounded abdomen.

Back of these waxplates and at the very tip of the bee's body is its sole means of defense against enemies — the sting. Without this weapon used to defend the collected honey, all the work of the bees would be undone. The sting is one of nature's wonders. It is sharp as the finest needle, almost as hard as steel, and barbed in the manner of a porcupine quill, so that once it enters it cannot be withdrawn. As the bee inserts the weapon into her enemy's body, she tries to free herself. By so doing she commits suicide since she pulls her body away from the sting which because of its barbs cannot be removed. A bee that stings you, then, kills herself in the act.

The queen has a curved sting without the barbs and so can use it over and over again, which she does on her rivals, about to be born or after their birth, in the fight for existence and supremacy which two queens will wage. Drones have no stings.

A hive of bees has from 30,000 to 50,000 or more members, the great majority working bees or neutral females, with the reproductive organs undeveloped. There is one queen to each hive and several hundred drones, allowed to live until the fall, when they are killed off. The bees act as if they know that winter is coming and they must conserve their food supply. The drones being unable or unwilling to work are an expensive nuisance, once their sole function—to fertilize the queen—has been performed. The "mind" of the working bees is on three things, nectar, pollen or flour, and propolis or glue. The industry of these creatures has always been a source of wonder to mankind. They literally kill themselves with hard work, and their brief span of working life is only about 30 or 40 days.

Honey to the hive represents life. It means food and warmth in months of cold. It is their liquid gold, without which they could not survive. The manner of production is most interesting. They collect the nectar with their hollow tongues inserted into the depths of the flowers, preferring always to stay with one kind of flower so as not to mix the flavors unduly, but nectar or the sweet tasting watery fluid which they are able to secure from the blossoms is far from being the honey which is so prized.

This thin fluid is taken into the honey bag or crop where the chemical factory begins to function. Complex chemical substances, known as enzymes, and believed to originate in the salivary or mouth glands, are mixed with the nectar. As the bee wings her way homeward the work goes on and the sugar of the nectar is being changed into the dextrose and levulose of honey.

On reaching the hive, the load of nectar is transferred to the crops of the younger workers. These bees work it in and out in a thorough mixing process until the mysterious chemical process is completed and now the partially ripened honey may be stored in the open six-sided cells. When the water has sufficiently evaporated to the satisfaction of the skilled bee-chemists and has arrived at the consistency and composition of honey, the cells are capped with a thin layer of wax. In these wax receptacles the honey keeps indefinitely, having had inserted into it a preservative which is the secret of the bee.

Honey is our most admirable carbohydrate food and has many uses. It consists of water, levulose, dextrose, cane sugar, dextrins and gums, with very small quantities of ash, beeswax, a few pollen grains, and coloring material from the plants supplying the nectar.

A newly-born bee after a few days in the hive is able to go out along with its fellow workers, carry out all the intricate operations of gathering honey, and the general work of the hive, without any instructions; they have received their knowledge before birth. Who, we ask again, could have been their Teacher?

Ordinary honey will flow rather freely, and the question arises, why does the honey not run out of the cells which are placed horizontally in the comb? The answer is that the bees, exhibiting an engineering skill which is the envy of humans, tilt their cells slightly upward in order, obviously, to keep the honey from running over the side.

The six-sided cells which make up the great bulk of the cells in the hive—only a few on the outer edges or in unusual spaces being triangular or square, or odd-shaped—are made with the greatest accuracy. In fact, so uniform is this size that some scientists have suggested that the cell of the hive bee be made the standard of measure.

The pollen or flour which the bees gather daily from the flowers is literally gold-dust to them. Rich in protein, it is fed to the early workers of the summer colony. The fertilization of plants depends principally on the work of these busy bees. If they were to be destroyed, there would be a famine in the land. So, the Creator has planned with great wisdom that these tiny insects should be of great use to mankind.

Propolis, the dark colored bee glue with which they fill cracks and smooth over rough places within the hive, is gathered from the gums of buds, plants and trees. It is a most effective varnish, and yet the bee seems never to be "stuck up" with it.

Wax is a product of the bees' chemical factory and comes from its body after the bees have gorged themselves with honey. It takes six or seven pounds of honey to make one pound of wax. This wax, after a series of preparations by the inmates of the hive, is secreted from the four centers on each side of the abdomen and appears as thin little plates looking like fish scales. It is removed by the hind legs, transferred to the middle pair, then to the mouth where it is mixed with saliva and changes from the transparent form it has when first secreted to the somewhat pale yellow color of the finished article.

In the wax there is evidence of design. It is unlike anything else in the world. It contains a fatty acid called cerin, minute quantities of alcohol, myricin, hydrocarbons, and another acid which gives the wax its characteristic odor.

It is lighter than water and floats. Very resistant to heat it will endure a temperature up to 140 degrees F. before it melts. No other wax has so high a melting point.

The reason for this high melting point can be easily understood. They would lose their whole store of liquid gold if the thin-walled treasure vaults, the storage chambers, softened under the influence of heat and gave way.

The mechanical engineering skill exercised in manipulating this wax into the cells excites our admiration and wonder. Apparently without a head engineer to advise or issue commands, one piece after another is laid down by the little workers, a tap here, and a dab there, and presently the cell takes shape. Who is responsible for all this intricate and precise operation? What is the "spirit of the hive" which Maeterlinck mentions? Is it not the Spirit of God?

There is not space to discuss all the marvellous operations of these insects, but we cannot close this study without thinking of the magic substance known as royal jelly. This miraculous substance, the product of the ductless glands of the nurse bees, the youngest in the colony, has some qualities which cannot be understood. All observers stand in amazement and awe when discussing the power of this food.

All baby bees—and when they are hatched from the eggs laid by the queen in the cells, they come forth as little white worms or grubs —are fed this jelly during the first 48 hours of their existence. Then a honey and pollen mixture replaces the royal jelly for drone and worker grubs. If a bee baby comes from a fertilized egg, that is, one in which the queen has placed a sperm derived from the drone husband, it could become a queen if fed royal jelly during its entire grub stage of life, a period of about five days. An unfertilized egg must develop into a drone. In other words a drone is virgin-born, having a mother but no father! And yet it has a grandfather. Those who talk about the biological impossibility of virgin birth had better go to the bee and learn!

The fact that the feeding of this royal jelly for five days—the larval life of the baby bee—changes the bee into a fully developed queen, with all the reproductive organs matured, is one of the great marvels of the world.

How do the bees know when they need a queen? How do they understand the changing of food and the mixing of pollen and honey in exact proportions day after day, as they urge their patients to eat incessantly in order to make use of the flying moments. One can imagine the nurses saying to the occupants of the rooms: "Hurry, baby, only four more days to eat—here is another meal—gorge yourself!"

About 1,300 meals daily are offered these grubs. Then, after five days they weave themselves a shroud—a silken winding sheet inside of which the mysterious change known as metamorphosis takes place—until the exciting day arrives when the fully-developed bee with wings and all the other equipment cuts through its wax covering and looks out on the new world.

It had been an egg for 3 days, then a

worm for 5, and from 12 to 14 inside its cocoon, in all 20-22 days.

For one or two days after birth, the bee is permitted to look around, and then having familiarized itself with its surroundings it gets to work. The first job assigned to it is the important one of feeding the babies that have been born at the rate of 1,000 or 1,500 daily, that many adult bees usually dying also. After a few days the nurses are promoted to the job of feeding the newly-born babies, previously having given their attention to the ones about two days old. After a week or ten days inside they become nectar gatherers, continuing that arduous life until with frayed and broken wings and exhausted bodies, they die at the age of 30 or 35 days.

Bees, in common with other cold-blooded creatures, have a temperature which is approximately that of the surrounding air. It has often been asked how the bees in winter, inside the hive, can manage to live. They adopt a unique method of avoiding death from freezing.

Their insect furnace begins to function when the temperature within the hive drops to about 57 degrees F. Then the bees gather in clusters and begin their dance in order to manufacture heat. They continually shift their position, night and day, passing from the center of the cluster to the outside where it is colder, moving and swaying, generating the necessary warmth. So effective is the system, that tests have shown a difference between the outside temperature and that inside of as much as 75 degrees. That is, when the cold is 10 degrees below zero outside, the bees are comfortable at 65 degrees above zero inside. Again, how do they have this knowledge?

We have touched on a few wonders of the bee. A thoughtful and intelligent person must come to certain conclusions when faced with these indisputable facts. The things which God has made reveal His divine Personality.

One or two more examples of remarkable animal instinct will be mentioned before we close this chapter. One is that of the beaver. In his book, "Organic Evolution Considered," Professor Fairhurst wrote:

"The beaver lives in communities and

constructs dams, sometimes as long as three hundred yards, stretching across shallow streams of water. These dams are built of sticks of wood, generally about three feet long and six or seven inches in diameter, which the animal cuts with its teeth.

"The sticks are put in the water and are held in position by means of mud, stones, and moss, which are placed upon them. The dams are ten or twelve feet thick at the base; and when the streams are wide the dams are made to curve upstream against the current, thus producing a structure better able to resist the force of the stream.

"The amount of labor necessary to construct a dam is enormous. Moreover, it requires an incredible number of logs of wood, and great skill in engineering. Near the dams the beavers build their houses. Each house is about seven feet in diameter in the interior, and three feet high in the center. The walls are of great thickness. Each lodge is large enough to accommodate five or six beavers. The outside is plastered with mud and carefully smoothed; and the mud is renewed each year in order to keep the house in good repair. All the houses of the colony are surrounded by a ditch which contains water; and each lodge is connected by a passageway with the ditch. As a supply of food for the winter, the beavers store up a large number of logs under the water, the bark of which they consume.

"Thus we find in this case an organized community, working for the common good, both in constructing the dam and the ditch, and also in storing up food; and then making special preparation for living in small groups by constructing their lodges and connecting them with the ditch.

"Here we see highly developed instincts which look to the future of the organism. The building of the dam, the digging of the ditch, the storing of the food, are all done to meet future emergencies. It is evident that the construction of the dam could not have been evolved gradually, for a dam must be of sufficient extent to be useful before Natural Selection could act.

"We are obliged to assume that in a single generation a beaver or colony of beavers was produced, which had a new instinct, sufficiently developed to enable them to build a useful dam; and that in consequence of this, they themselves were the better preserved; and that the instinct was transmitted to the offspring. If all this could have happened in a single generation, it is evident that no question need be raised as to the possibility of future evolution. Besides this, the construction of a ditch for water around the several lodges required a different instinct, serving a purpose. Its evolution involves similar difficulties."

The case of the water spider as recorded by Graebner in "God and the Cosmos" is worthy of note. We quote:

"We ask ourselves if there be any conceivable way in which its peculiar instincts and manner of life could have been derived, by instinct, from others of the spider family. Like other spiders the water spider is an air-breathing animal, yet unlike other spiders, it lives under water.

"How did it evolve the extraordinary changes in its organism, and in its habits of life, whereby it acquired first, its set purpose to live under water; and second, its special organs and instincts, whereby it is enabled to give effect to that strange purpose, and to live, thrive, and rear its young in such unnatural environment?

"In order to live under water, and rear its young there, it must construct a waterproof cell, capable of containing enough air for breathing purposes; it must have means for renewing the supply of air from time to time; and it must have the instincts to guide in the performance of these necessary operations. And we may confidently add that the very first water spider must have been fully equipped for the purposes indicated. It spins under water an egg-shaped envelope, open underneath for entrance and egress. This envelope which is waterproof, is securely attached to some object so that it will remain submerged.

"Having constructed its house, the little creature next proceeds to fill it with air. For this necessary operation, its hind legs are covered with hair and are so constructed that they can take hold of a large bubble of air, and carry it down into the water, and to the opening of its house. There the air is released, and it rises to the top of the envelope, expelling the corresponding quantity of water.

"This operation is repeated until the cell is sufficiently filled with air. The eggs are then laid in the upper part of the house and are then surrounded by a cocoon.

"Philip Mauro in his book 'Evolution at the Bar,' fitly remarks: 'It is manifest that this extraordinary manner of life, and the highly specialized organs, which are vital to it, could not possibly be the outcome of a long and slow process of evolution. Before the life of a water spider could begin, it must be equipped, first, with the means of secreting a waterproof material; second, means for spinning that material into a watertight cell; third, protective hairs to keep it from becoming wet; fourth, the peculiar apparatus for filling its house with air; fifth, the several instincts which prompt the doing of these remarkable things.'"

The animal world is literally full of all kinds of similar wonders, each species showing its own peculiar set of instincts and equipment. The actions are performed more or less blindly, without any instruction, and are as perfect at the first attempt as at the last. There can be but one explanation of these remarkable gifts and that explanation is creation.

CHAPTER NINE

THE HUMAN BODY

Even a slight acquaintance with the structure and operations of the human body machine will convince the open-minded student that evidence abounds of the presence of plan and foresight. Everywhere we touch it we are confronted with these proofs. The author's book, "God and You"* will repay close reading. It describes in some detail many remarkable features associated with the body.

In this chapter will be mentioned a small number of interesting items for which there can be no explanation other than that which has been adduced so many times in this book —a personal God.

Paley, while lacking much knowledge which is today available, nevertheless draws attention in a convincing manner to many points

---
*Fundamental Truth Publishers, Findlay, O., Price, $1.00.

which are often overlooked. The mechanical arrangement of the bony skeleton is altogether worthy of study.

In the human neck two things must be provided for. The head must have the power to bend forward and backward, as in the act of nodding, stooping, looking up or down; also it is required to turn itself upon the body, to the right and to the left. For these two purposes two distinct contrivances are employed. The skull rests on the upper or first cervical vertebra and is united to it by a double joint. On this joint the head plays freely forward and backward, and from side to side, as far as necessary, or as far as the ligaments permit.

But this does not take care of the rotatory motion. Therefore, a further mechanism is introduced. This is between the first and second vertebrae. This second bone, called the axis, the first being known as the atlas, has a process similar in size and shape to a large eye-tooth. This tooth enters a corresponding socket in the atlas above it, forming a pivot or axle upon which the upper bone together with the skull it supports, turns freely in a circular manner. This movement is limited and checked by attached ligaments specially designed for this purpose.

When we nod the head we use the double joint which lies between the skull and first vertebra. When we turn the head, the pivot joint is used, between the first and second neck bones.

An obvious reason why the motion of the head forward and backward should be performed between the skull and first neck bone, is that if the first vertebra itself had bent forward, the spinal cord would be injured by the projecting tooth of the second vertebra.

The spinal column or backbone is a chain of bones and joints very wonderfully constructed. Many uses must be planned for here. It must be firm to support the erect position of the body and also flexible to allow of the bending of the trunk in all degrees of curvature. It must form a tube or channel in the bones for conveying with perfect safety the delicate but immensely important spinal cord, injury of which or any unusual pressure upon, is followed by paralysis or death.

Not only must the spine furnish the canal for the spinal cord, but it must have openings for the exit of nerves all along its course, supplying all parts of the body. In addition it must provide attachment for many muscles to act upon this long lever or movable column. And lastly, it must furnish a proper support on which the ends of the ribs may rest.

The manner in which the twenty-four bones of the spine are connected is a beautiful example of perfect mechanical work. Between each pair of bones is a wonderful layer of elastic cartilage, preventing injury and shock on the principle of rubber heels. A hole is bored in each bone, each opening fitting accurately the one above and the one below, so that a perfect canal is formed. Small openings permit the egress of the spinal nerves and the whole contrivance is held together very firmly by strong ligaments which effectively prevent dislocation or injury, unless there is actual fracture of the bones from a severe injury.

When the spine is viewed as a whole it is observed to become gradually thicker and stronger from above downwards, the interlocking of the bones successively closer; obviously designed to sustain the accumulating weight, and to prevent fracture at the point of greatest risk—the lower part.

In the curves of the spinal column we find an interesting arrangement. At the top the neck bones curve forward, then in the dorsal region, the curve is backward, and in the lower or lumbar area, the curve is again forward. How logical and prearranged this is!

The backward curve in the dorsal region provides greater space for the organs of the chest; strength is given by the ease with which these curves yield under the pressure and shock to the brain is prevented by the curves and the buffers in between each pair of bones. The jar from running and jumping is very materially lessened.

The entire column is firmly fixed on the central bone of the pelvis, the weight being distributed through an irregular arch of bone on either side, to the lower extremities. It can easily be seen that the general result is admirable. All movements of the body are performed easily and safely so that a contortionist is able to twist himself into impossible positions without any harm resulting. The evidence of design is overwhelming.

Every joint is a mechanical curiosity. Joints are of two kinds, hinge, and ball-and-socket. These are beautifully constructed and of course adapted to the motion required in each particular place. Strong ligaments extend over and around the ends of the bones, keeping the corresponding parts of the joint in close application to each other.

The pliability and firmness of these articulations awaken our admiration. In all moveable joints the ends of the bones are covered with cartilage, a smooth, elastic material exactly suited to its use, diminishing jarring and preventing the wearing away of the ends of the bones. In some joints, notably the knee-joints, these cartilages are loose rings, a device of modern mechanics.

One of the most arresting features of joints is the method of lubrication, the joint itself manufacturing the finest kind of oil known—the synovial fluid, more emollient than any other known oil, and providing a perfect lubricant constantly operating while the joint is in use, and without any attention from the possessor of the joints, except that he continue to use them.

Muscles with their tendons are the instruments by which motion is made possible. There is always an exact relation between the joint and the muscles which move it. Whatever motion the joint can perform will be produced by the associated muscles.

There are some very curious muscles. For instance, the sartorious or tailor's muscle which rises from the pelvis and runs diagonally across the thigh, taking hold of the tibia, the inside bone of the leg, a little below the knee. By its contraction or shortening—the peculiar way in which muscle operates—one leg can be thrown over the other, the thigh rolling outward, giving effect at the same time to the ball-and-socket joint at the hip, and the knee-joint at the knee.

Muscles are so placed that they do not obstruct or interfere with one another's action. When we remember that the body has some

520 muscles, lying close to each other, in layers over one another, crossing one another, sometimes embedded in another, sometimes perforating another, we must be convinced of a designed arrangement.

The human tongue is made up of many muscles twining and intertwining in an astonishing way. This arrangement makes possible many varied motions performed swiftly and with great precision. Paley writes:

> "It is worth any man's while to watch the agility of his tongue; the wonderful promptitude with which it executes change of position, and the perfect exactness. Each syllable of articulated sound requires for its utterance a specific action of the tongue, and of the parts adjacent to it. The disposition and configuration of the mouth for every letter and word is not only peculiar, but if nicely and accurately attended to, perceptible to the sight. . . . How instantaneously are these positions assumed and dismissed! how numerous are the permutations, how various, yet how infallible!"

There are some single muscles which bear marks of wise contrivance. One of these is the muscle which pulls down the lower jaw.

The obvious method which would occur to a human mechanic would be to fix a muscle between the chin and top of the chest—say on the collarbone. The shortening of this muscle would pull down the lower jaw. But the configuration of the neck would be spoiled so the artistry of God caused Him to devise an ingenious substitute. The muscle which actually does the work is called the digastric, and is attached behind the ear to the mastoid bone. It would appear at first glance that this descending muscle would act by elevating the jaw, and not by depressing it. But how simple and clever is the device. When the descending tendon gets low enough it is passed through a loop or pulley in the hyoid bone of the neck, and then made to turn upward. Its final insertion is into the bone on the inner side of the chin. By this curious device the muscle in its contraction or shortening performs its destined job perfectly,—pulling the jaw down and not up.

An interesting mechanical contrivance found in some muscles is where one tendon passes through a slit in another tendon, as with the tendons which move the fingers and toes. The long tendon in the foot, for instance, which bends the first joint of the toe, passes through the short tendon which bends the second joint. This gives freedom of action which otherwise would not have been possible. This must have been planned.

And we cannot refrain from calling attention to another strong proof of design in the ligament or strap which binds down the tendons at the ankle, passing from the leg down to the foot. The foot is placed at a considerable angle to the leg. The flexible tendons passing along the interior or front of the angle if left to themselves would spring forward when stretched. The obvious device is to tie them down. So, across the instep or just above it there is a strong ligamentous band under which the tendons pass to the foot. If this is cut, there is immediate disfigurement of the part when the muscles act.

There is space for but one more wonder of the human body as evidence of a Master-workman. Let us look briefly at the most remarkable camera—the eye.

Dr. Theodore Graebner in "God and the Cosmos," pp. 40, 41 puts the points so clearly and concisely that we can do no better than quote his description:

"In order to see anything clearly, it is necessary that an image or picture of it should be formed at the back of the eye, that is, on the retina from whence the impression is communicated to the brain. The eye is an instrument used for producing the picture, and in some respects, is very similar to a telescope. In both eye and telescope the rays of light have to be refracted (or bent) so as to produce a distinct image; the lens and humors in the eye effect this.

"The different humors through which the rays pass prevent them from being partly split up into different colors.

"In the next place, the eye has to be suited to perceive objects at different distances, varying from inches to miles. This is done by slightly altering the shape of the lens, making it more or less convex. A landscape of several miles is thus brought within a space of half an inch in diameter, though the objects it contains, at least the larger ones, are all preserved, and can each be distinguished in its size, shape, color, and position. Yet the same eye that can do this can read a book at a distance of a few inches.

"The remarkable thing about the eye is the retina, an enlargement and specialization of the optic nerve. This retina is composed of eleven layers, the tenth of which is 'Jacob's membrane,' in which the rods and cones, peculiarly adapted to receiving vibrations of light, give us the sense of color. Without these rods and cones . . . all the world would appear as a monotonous outline, for there is no color in the objects themselves. Every object gives off a different vibration of light, and when these vibrations reach the rods and cones they stimulate the optic nerve, which carries the impression through half a dozen portals to the visual center in the back of the brain, where we see the objects in their various colors. The impression of design seems inevitable when we consider the mosaic of the human retina, with its elements regularly arranged, and set at distances of only one or two ten-thousandths of an inch apart, and think of these almost countless elements destined to convey the impressions of the almost countless points which we distinguish as separate in the field of view.

"Again the eye has to be adapted to different degrees of light. This is done by the iris, which is a kind of screen in the shape of a ring, capable of expanding or contracting so as to alter the size of the central hole or pupil, yet always retaining its central form.

"Moreover it is somehow self-adjusting; if the light is too strong, the pupil (or shutter of the camera) at once contracts. . . .

"Once more, the eye can perceive objects in different directions; it is so constructed that it can turn with the greatest rapidity right or left, up or down, without moving the head.

"It is also provided in duplicate, the two eyes being so arranged that though each can see separately . . . they can see together in perfect harmony.

"On the whole then, the eye appears to be an optical instrument of great ingenuity; and the conclusion that it must have been made by someone, and that whoever made it must have known and designed its use, seems inevitable.

"All the various and complicated parts of the eye agree in this remarkable point, and in this one only, that they enable man to see; and it is this that requires explanation. We feel that there must be some connection between the cause which brought all these parts together and the fact of man's seeing. In other words, the result must have been designed.

"But the argument is far stronger than this. We remember that the eye was formed before birth. It was of no use when it was made, it was intended for the future; this, when carefully considered, shows design more plainly than anything else.

"Moreover, an eye is found not in one man only, but in millions of men, each separately showing marks of design, and each separately requiring a designer.

"The human eye is only one example out of hundreds in the human body. The ear or mouth would lead to the same conclusion, and so would the lungs or the heart.

"Finally, human beings are but one of many thousands of organisms in nature, all bearing marks of design, and showing in some cases an even greater ingenuity than the human eye."

The above is a strong presentation of a few of the mysteries of the eye. By no means has this brief discussion exhausted the manifest marvels of this structure. But surely there can be but one inescapable inference. The impact of all this evidence ought to bring a conviction of the existence of the great God who is the subject of our closing chapter.

CHAPTER TEN

SEEING GOD

The preceding chapters have been written with but one end in view—that the reader may come in his thinking to a sure conviction in regard to the existence of a personal and loving Creator. That conception which makes of God a hazy, indefinite, blindly-operating, omnipotent Force is supported neither by the Bible nor by the innumerable facts available to us in every realm of nature.

The important truth of the personality of God meets us on every page of Scripture. Our Heavenly Father has tried to give us a conception of Himself within the limits of our finite understanding. This picture painted from differing viewpoints and in varying colors is not complete, but is surely sufficient for our present needs. As we study it, we are led to a certain knowledge that He is, and also that He covets and enjoys our fellowship.

We read that we are made "in the image of God and after His likeness." That means that we have some of God's characteristics. It implies also that He possesses some of our qualities—but in infinite measure. He has a mind capable of infinite perceptions. He thinks, plans, loves, hates, remembers, and even forgets. He tells us that He "will not remember" our sins (Isa. 43:25).

All of God's powers, because of infinite degree, are beyond our complete understanding, but that does not prevent us from making His acquaintance. We may know Him because He is a Person who has revealed Himself as clearly as our finite qualities can grasp. Our limited capacities cannot penetrate far, but far enough for us to say with Paul: "I know whom I have believed." And with Job we cry: "I know that my Redeemer liveth."

That which can plan and design must be a person, for this ability implies consciousness and thought. These acts require a mind which can perceive and will. Wherever there is a person there is a mind; wherever there is mind there must be a person to use and control it.

To say that all things have come because of the working of certain inexorable laws, and to deny that these laws need a Lawgiver is an illogically absurd proposition. A law presupposes an agent for the law is only the manner according to which the agent proceeds. It also implies a power for it is the order according to which the power acts. Without this agent, without this power, which are both distinct from itself, the law does nothing, is nothing.

Not only do we know of the existence of Deity but we are able to determine some of His attributes. It is a supreme conclusion that there is a God—a perceiving, intelligent, designing Being, at the head of creation, and from whose will it proceeded.

The attributes of such a Being must accord with the magnitude, extent, and variety of His operations. These operations are not only vast beyond comparison with those performed by any other power, but so far as our conception of them, they are infinite because unlimited on all sides.

The contemplation of so exalted a nature overwhelms our faculties. Our minds feel their inability to understand the infinitude of such a Person. We must think of Him in terms of superlatives. We speak of His eternity, omnipotence, omniscience, omnipresence.

The human mind is helpless before the thought of God's timelessness. When we read Psalm 90:2, and our imaginations project themselves into the undated past we are lost in the tremendous idea that God had no beginning:

> "Before the mountains were brought forth, or ever Thou hadst formed the earth and the world, even from everlasting to everlasting, Thou art God." (Psa. 90:2.)

Where we are unable to understand we must simply believe. That ought not to be difficult since we are constantly accepting many lesser things which we do not understand.

> "But will God indeed dwell upon the earth? Behold the heaven and the heaven

of heavens cannot contain Thee." (I Kings 8:27.)

"Canst thou by searching find out God? Canst thou find the Almighty unto perfection? It is high as heaven; what canst thou do? Deeper than Sheol; what canst thou know? The measure thereof is longer than the earth, and broader than the sea." (Job 11:7-9.)

The superlative knowledge and wisdom of God we call omniscience.

"Great is our Lord and of great power; His understanding is infinite." (Psa. 147:5.)

There are no unanswered questions or problems with God. Man has just touched the fringe of the vast ocean of knowledge but our God is the source of all things. One of the glories of coming days will be the joy of discovering the answer to those questions which have always occupied the human mind, and about which we know practically nothing. It seems that Socrates was not far wrong when he is said to have remarked: "The only thing we know is that we do not know anything."

We come to realize as we study the varied

and intricate activities of our God something of His omnipresence.

> "Can any hide himself from Me in secret places that I shall not see him, saith the Lord? Do not I fill heaven and earth, saith the Lord?" (Jer. 23:24.)

It is one thing to recognize the existence of God and quite another to realize His nearness to us and His accessibility. So many Christians have not had the joy of His daily presence. Even in prayer, many acknowledge there is little appreciation of any intimate fellowship with a Person. This lack is what makes our prayers so perfunctory and formal. A sense of communicating directly with this Supreme Being will immediately change the tenor of our supplications and bring a thrill which is not possible in any other experience. It is fine to know about our Lord, but how much better really to know Himself. We are sure that God lives—are we just as certain that He lives IN US?

The immutability, the justice, the absolute holiness of God are qualities that intrigue our minds when we think of our wonderful Father.

To know that one day we shall be like Christ in reality makes us long for that glad day when we shall be with Him.

Our final consideration is of the goodness of God. All that we have seen and all that we know reflects this quality of love. This love of God is manifest in creation, in all the benefits He devised for us, and in the pleasures He makes possible for us. Truly it is a fact that "He gives us all things richly to enjoy."

After all, this is a happy world. The earth, the air, and the water teem with creatures taking great delight in their existence. Wherever one looks, myriads of happy beings crowd upon our view. On any summer evening, swarms of newborn flies are trying their wings in air, A honeybee among the flowers is one of the most cheerful objects in nature. The whole winged insect world are equally intent upon their proper employments. All types of life wherever found exhibit a vivacious enjoyment of life, however brief, that ought to teach us many a lesson.

We are overwhelmed with the abounding mercies of God and as we take another look at the FOOTPRINTS OF GOD, we are led to exclaim with the Psalmist:

> "Oh, come, let us sing unto the Lord; let us make a joyful noise to the rock of our salvation. Let us come before His presence with thanksgiving; let us make a joyful noise unto Him with psalms. For the Lord is a great God, and a great king above all gods.....
>
> O come, let us worship and bow down; let us kneel before the Lord our Maker: FOR HE IS OUR GOD and we are the people of His pasture, and the sheep of His hand.
>
> Today, oh, that you would hear His voice...." (Psa. 95.)

> "Bless the Lord, O my soul. O Lord my God, Thou art very great; Thou art clothed with honor and majesty: who covereth Thyself with light as with a garment....
>
> O Lord, how manifold are Thy works! In wisdom hast Thou made them all: the earth is full of Thy riches....
>
> I will sing unto the Lord as long as I live: I will sing praise to my God while I have any being; let my meditation be sweet unto Him: I will rejoice in the Lord." (Psalm 104.)

FOOTPRINTS OF GOD 245

If the reader has followed the author thus far he will not need to be informed that the purpose of this writing is to exalt the Creator. It is an inspiring and magnificent Truth that Jesus Christ—the Man of Galilee—and now the "Forgotten Man"—almost—is the One who brought all things into existence. The "Man of Galilee" is the omnipotent Son of God and we read in Colossians 1:16: "In Him were all things created."

It is no wonder that the Holy Spirit asks in Isaiah 53:1 — "Who hath believed our report?" The wonder of a physical creation fades into insignificance when compared to the wonder of the creation of children of God through faith in the atoning blood of the Son of God. The plan and story of Redemption, to the natural man, is impossible and utterly fantastic, but, nevertheless it is true.

"He was made sin for us who knew no sin, that we might be made the righteousness of God in Him." Intelligence demands that we accept Jesus Christ as the Supreme Creator of all things. It ought not to be hard to go a little further and believe that if He could perform all the miracles associated with that monumental work, He can save every lost and guilty sinner who comes to Him confessing sin and is willing to accept the substitutionary sacrifice of our wonderful Lord.

Reader, have you done this? If not—why not **now**?